IMBIBING *for* INTROVERTS

IMBIBING for INTROVERTS

A Guide to Social Drinking for the Anti-Social

JEFF CIOLETTI

author of *The Drinkable Globe*

Skyhorse Publishing

Skyhorse Publishing books may be purchased in bulk at special discounts for sales promotion, corporate gifts, fund-raising, or educational purposes. Special editions can also be created to specifications. For details, contact the Special Sales Department, Skyhorse Publishing, 307 West 36th Street, 11th Floor, New York, NY 10018 or info@skyhorsepublishing.com.

Skyhorse® and Skyhorse Publishing® are registered trademarks of Skyhorse Publishing, Inc.®, a Delaware corporation.

Visit our website at www.skyhorsepublishing.com.

10 9 8 7 6 5 4 3 2 1

Library of Congress Cataloging-in-Publication Data is available on file.

Cover design by David Ter-Avanesyan
Cover illustration by Elena Makansi
Interior design and layout by Chris Schultz

Print ISBN: 978-1-5107-6827-7
Ebook ISBN: 978-1-5107-6828-4

Printed in China

For my wife, Craige, who's far more extroverted than I'll ever be.

TABLE OF CONTENTS

PART I

DEFINING INTROVERSION & LOVING IT AT HOME

INTRODUCTION

I DRINK ALONE

(BUT NOT IN A SELF-DESTRUCTIVE, GEORGE THOROGOOD KIND OF WAY)

I have a love/hate relationship with dinner parties. And I wouldn't say that's a 50/50 relationship, more like a 20/80 situation. Okay, maybe 10/90.

It's always great when someone invites you to one and it feels pretty sucky to be excluded from a guest list, but it's an activity that almost always looks better on paper.

Don't get me wrong. Dinner parties are fine if you know the majority of the people there and the group is limited to six or eight, tops. But more often than not, they involve a DeMille-ian cast of thousands, primarily so the hosts can show off just how popular they are. And, invariably, you're going to be seated next to someone you don't know (or, worse, don't like), with whom you have zero chemistry or common ground.

And the notion of a "group conversation" is a myth. When you're stuck with more than a half-dozen people at a table, it's next to impossible to carry on a discussion with anyone who's not sitting next to or directly across from you, so it all just devolves into a collection of micro-chats over which you have little control.

This is also true of wedding receptions—of the sit-down-meal variety. It's unfathomable to me why we allow the dubious seating chart decisions of distant relatives or casual acquaintances dictate the kind of evening we're going to have and how much or how little we're going to enjoy the celebration. (Spoiler alert: nobody cares about this event nearly as much as the brides and grooms, and perhaps their very immediate family and closest friends—who are likely bridesmaids or groomsmen to begin with and completely hammered before they even arrive at the banquet hall). No matter how successful the nuptials are, Murphy's Law requires us to be stuck at a twelve-top table immediately adjacent to the dullest or most bigoted human being imaginable.

Things get progressively worse if you're not clicking with your forced companion and you inevitably reach that treacherous conversational fork in the road: small talk or absolute silence. Those options always remind me of a quote from *Doctor Who*: "Sometimes the only choices are bad ones. But you still have to choose." I'd much rather choose silence over small talk seven days a week, but societal pressures disallow it. Being branded "anti-social" or, God forbid, "a little off" can sting with the force of one thousand murder hornets—especially if you're someone like me who tries to construct a façade as someone who's "above it all" and "doesn't give a shit what other people think" but is really pathologically desperate for the approval of strangers.

Playing the Extroversion Game is exhausting for those of us on the opposite end of the socialization spectrum, but it's a game in which we nonetheless engage more frequently than most of us would like.

As a journalist who exclusively covers beverages, I find myself in these sorts of situations an above-average number of times, as any major industry events—trade shows, tastings, conferences, brand launches, or any combination thereof—usually come with the obligatory media dinners/dog-and-pony shows. To be sure, I typically look forward to such invitations because they tend to be at upscale restaurants on somebody else's dime (look up "median income of trade journalist" if you have any questions as to why). When I discover they're going to be plated meals and not eat-and-run buffets or "heavy hors d'oeuvres," "I'll make a ten-minute appearance"-style soirees, that's when the panic sets in and the perspiration commences. But thank God these are *booze* events, at which imbibing is not only expected, but pretty much mandatory. Not because I can drink myself into oblivion (I never do that and don't recommend it) but because I can retreat into "contemplation and evaluation" mode, where I jot down notes after every sip. I might be scribbling gibberish—as I very often am—but it makes a nice suit of armor during these unnecessarily intense moments. I look like "Mr. Serious Journalist" for a few minutes, something with which other media folk who RSVP'd for the junket can absolutely relate.

I also don't do too well at cocktail parties (see: talk, small) and my characteristic posture at said gatherings is hunched over a corner high-boy table attempting to photograph (is that term still relevant in the post-digital age?) my drink from every possible angle, and then spending the next twenty or so minutes posting it—with every vaguely appropriate hashtag—to multiple Instagram and Twitter accounts. There are times when I notice out of the corner of my eye that other attendees are approaching my one-man base camp—it's not like you can lick a table and claim it as your own—and the "gracefully escape" window closes too quickly. In those instances, I'll type and chuckle intermittently at my screen as if I'm engaged in my own virtual conversation. (That technique works far less than I'd hope because, practically without fail, the uninvited interloper will crane their neck to try to read my name badge and then confidently announce that the network-y interrogation is about to begin with the words, "Who are you with?")

Look, I don't dislike conversations per se, even with strangers. I just believe, like friendships, they need to develop organically and not in some kind of contrived manner, preordained by the conventions of the particular social setting.

The most excruciating examples in said environments involve some kind of icebreaker to obliquely declare, "now is time in party when we talk." I was at a whiskey event in New Orleans once when one of the brand reps floated through six or seven connecting rooms with a Mad Libs pad, trying to strong-arm the guests into playing along. As the kids say, "Cringe!" Forced fun at its absolute worst—and I clearly wasn't the only one who thought so because the responses were less than enthusiastic.

If you're still reading and haven't reached the conclusion that I'm an absolutely terrible person, I can assure you that I don't hate people. Quite the contrary, I love them quite a bit. (After all, I count myself among them!)

But my affection for humanity parallels my affinity for fine drink: everything in moderation.

Having to perpetually be "on" in the presence of other carbon-based life-forms is mentally and emotionally taxing and I require at least an equal amount of time in decompression mode. And that very often involves a complex, lovingly crafted adult beverage.

Please do not interpret this as "social interactions drive me to drink." Such a take stems, unfortunately, from the stigma that has been placed on drinking alone. Alcohol-based drinks should not be a means to an end—that undesirable end being inebriation. They're an end in themselves—a reward, a "treat yourself" moment, to steal a concept from *Parks & Recreation*. It's not about the effects, it's about the ritual. As my wife would enthusiastically tell you, I'm a notorious "lightweight." To the untrained eye, I'm someone who will sit and nurse the same beverage for hours at a time. But I'm not nursing. I'm savoring—and not just the liquid in the glass, but my thoughts, the environment in which I'm consuming it, and the overall moment. I do enjoy social drinks with friends and loved ones—but no more than two or three other people at a time, please!

If any of this sounds even remotely familiar to you, you very well might be an introvert. Congratulations! As the onslaught of memes in your Facebook feed likely will tell you, it is finally our time. That means it's our time to have the time of our lives. And the pages that follow will help you lean into it.

Now, before we go any further, I must issue a disclaimer: I am not any sort of mental health professional. Aside from an aborted attempt at majoring in psychology in the nineties—I switched my major to a double in journalism and political science midstream—I have zero training in brain stuff. I only have my lifelong experience as a mostly undiagnosed introvert to go on here, so if you're looking for some sort of psychiatric self-help book, this ain't it. I fancy myself more of an evangelist for elevated drinking culture than anything that requires a license to operate professionally (except, of course, my driver's license, which affirms that I am of legal consumption age).

But you know who is an accredited professional? Jonathan M. Cheek, PhD, professor of psychology at Wellesley College in Massachusetts. Dr. Cheek is responsible for some of the most seminal work on introversion and he generously has provided a bit of his expert insight for this book. He's best known for identifying the four types of introvert: Social, Thinking, Anxious, and Restrained. Social Introverts prefer small gatherings over large ones and greatly value their alone time. Then there's the Thinking Introvert, who tends to get very introspective during social situations. Anxious Introverts, as you'd expect, typically avoid many social interactions due to their anxiety.

And Restrained Introverts exhibit a more reserved nature when they're around other people.

Dr. Cheek is quick to offer the caveat that these aren't necessarily four mutually exclusive classifications. There could be some overlap, with some shades of the others trickling into whichever one (or two) may dominate a particular individual's personality. Think of it as X-Y, horizontal and vertical axes with four quadrants, each quadrant representing one of the types of introversion. "I think it's a very useful way of analysis, but I don't think it's the test that rules the world," Cheek admits. "It's more like your individual profile in a way. Most introverts have some of each, but they may be more pronounced on one." Let's dive a little deeper into those and see how drops or splashes of each can be present in the same human being.

"Social introversion is often called 'preference for solitude,' although it's really a 'preference for a few familiar people' kind of thing," Dr. Cheek tells me, mentioning the title of Thomas Hardy's 1874 novel *Far from the Madding Crowd* as the sort of vibe social introverts seek. To this, I can relate 1,000 percent. "Mostly, humans are social animals, expressed in different ways," he explains. "Really, it's about a few familiar people that you have shared values or interests or social compatibility with." It's not that they're anti-social, he says, "they're just anti-crowds, anti-noisy crowds." I definitely tick that box.

When it comes to the Thinking Introvert, another apt term would be contemplative. "It tends to be a self-reflective, rich inner life," Cheek explains. That certainly carries over to their drinking experiences: "It could be . . . certain kinds of bourbon. It's an introspectiveness, a contemplativeness, drinking rituals that are appreciating the thing, savoring, going slowly."

Those are honestly my favorite moments, so I definitely have some elements within this category.

Anxious Introverts, meanwhile, might not be able to relax quite enough to allow in those moments of quiet contemplation. They want to maintain control of their situation and will often find ways to adapt to refocus their anxiety. This one can sometimes hit home with me as well. I mention my penchant for aggressively taking notes and pictures at cocktail parties and other meet-and-greet scenarios. "That's a coping strategy," Cheek informs me when I tell him about these tendencies. "That could work well for any introvert. Introverts would probably be happiest to have something to do like that as an anxiety reducer."

But sometimes for me, the lines can be blurred between the Anxious and the Restrained Introvert. I'm not necessarily retreating into my anxiety. I could be just (subconsciously) waiting for the right social window. I'm often mistaken for shy or even rude sometimes. The moment I find the right comfort level with others—or the right comfort level finds me—you can't shut me up. "There's actually some old social psychology lab research where it shows that if you can get a shy person comfortable in a situation, they'll talk more than the not-shy people," Cheek says, "because they suddenly got the opportunity."

Now, about that word "shy." "My first study on introversion was a study to try to separate shy people from non-Anxious Introverts," he recalls. "So, there were some introverts who were just social introverts, and they were not anxious. Prior to that, that [distinction] couldn't ever be identified. There was just a lot of conflation and confusion, with shy and introverted used as synonyms." Equating the two really pisses off a lot of introverts. One such person was a student of Cheek's who did her entire honors thesis on that subject. "She was so tired of people saying to her, 'Oh, I finally got a chance to talk to you, it must be hard for you being so shy.' She would get mad [and say] 'There's nothing shy about me, I'm just an introvert. I don't want to be chatting and meeting new people all the time.'"

Can I get an "Amen"?

DON'T MAKE ME GO OUT THERE

(OR, THE JOYS OF A HOME BAR)

If there's one thing the Great Pandemic has taught me it's that I really don't mind being home. While seemingly everyone in the social media-sphere was aching for human contact, I just, sort of, leaned into being home. Sure, I'm married and all and valued the extra time I got to spend with my wife (heh, really!), but I equally valued the moments I had to myself when she was off doing a wine Zoom with friends or a virtual office happy hour. She might have a different take on that, since it meant I descended deeper into my recently acquired vinyl LP addiction and, in the process, chipped away at what little nest egg we may have had.

When I wasn't disposing of my (barely) disposable income on 33⅓ and 45 rpm flat circles from Discogs.com and Crooked Beat Records in Alexandria, Virginia (shout-out to Bill), I was bingeing whatever series or movies my wife didn't want to watch with me. This included complete rewatches of all nine seasons of *The Office* (the American one) and all seven seasons of *Parks & Recreation*, two separate multipart documentaries on Keith Raniere's NXVIM sex cult, Amazon Prime's batshit crazy superhero saga *The Boys*, and the epic *Karate Kid* reboot, *Cobra Kai*. (I'm grateful every day that COVID-19 didn't happen in the eighties or nineties. I think I would've gone full Colonel Kurtz—*Apocalypse Now*—if streaming wasn't yet a thing.)

I, like my wife, have done my share of Zoom (un)happy hours, but those get old really quickly (I'm sure I don't need to tell any of you that). And that's mainly because they're not set up to be intimate social gatherings, composed of a patchwork of smaller conversations that enhance the greater umbrella event. In the virtual milieu, you can't have a mini discussion like you would with the individual seated next to/across from you at a larger table or booth. Instead, you have to stare at the "Hollywood Squares" of folks on your laptop screen and wait your turn to talk *at* everyone. If this is supposed to be fun, why is the vibe no different than that of giving a PowerPoint presentation in a conference room?

When I'm imbibing at home, the only people I want to be drinking with are my good friends Netflix, Hulu, and U-Turn Audio (the brand of turntable I own, if that wasn't clear).

And for everything, there is a beverage—whatever kind of mood you're in tonight (thanks, Billy).

Tuning Out & Entertaining Yourself

My own personal home bar is located just a few feet from my vinyl record collection—and that's by design (well, okay, it's more of a co-incidence). And I want neither to ever collect dust. So, it's time to get spinning (and yes, streamed music and MP3s are absolutely welcome if you lack a turntable). Since everyone's tastes are different, I'm going to stick with pairings for musical genres, rather than individual artists/records.

Surf Rock

Regrettably, I am a relatively recent convert to surf music and feel like such a poser when I attend shows with far more seasoned fans—which is why I prefer listening to my increasingly vast collection of reverb-enhanced, ocean-inspired, guitar-based instrumentals alone at home, far from the judgment of surfier-than-thou audience members (which, admittedly, exists primarily in my own head).

My entry point into the genre was actually through booze, so it's a total no-brainer when it comes to drink pairing. When I was researching my first book, *The Year of Drinking Adventurously*, I immersed myself fully in the tiki subculture. So much so, that I never left.

Surf rock is one of the many sub-subcultures within that world and, incidentally, the music that convinced me to procure the first record player that I'd owned in nearly thirty years. (I got the four members of the all-women, Toronto-based band The Surfrajettes to sign their 7-inch 45 rpm vinyl months before I even had the aforementioned turntable).

So, whether we're talking classic, first-wave artists like Dick Dale, the Ventures, the Lively Ones, the Sentinals, and the Tornadoes or revivalists like Satan's Pilgrims (RIP, Dave), the Surfrajettes, Messer Chups, the Surfites, Black Flamingos, the Delstroyers, and Didi Wray, the tunes sound much better when there's something like a Zombie or a Mai Tai in your hand (preferably in a charming mug with all the right garnishes and tchotchkes sticking out of it).

MARACUYA PISCO SOUR

Serves: 2

I wouldn't call a pisco sour a tiki drink per se (there will be some of those in the tiki chapter of this book), but the maracuya really brings it into that realm. Maracuya is just the Spanish term for passion fruit. I'm keeping it in that language because it comes to me via one of my favorite surf rock guitarists, Didi Wray. Didi (real name: Melina Sarmiento), who hails from Argentina and currently resides in Chile, infuses some of her homeland in her music, performing what she calls "surf tango." Her Peruvian friend Diego Ugaz turned her on to the maracuya version of his home country's national cocktail.

3 ounces pisco

¼ cup simple syrup

juice of 1 lime

1 ounce passion fruit juice

1 egg white

7 ice cubes

4 dashes bitters

Add pisco, simple syrup, juices, egg white, and ice cubes into a blender and blend. Pour into two sour glasses. Put two dashes of bitters on the surface of each of the drinks.

JACK THE RIPPER

Serves: 1

I'm including this one because it reminds me of Link Wray, whose guitar style was greatly influential on the surf rock movement (he's often considered "proto-surf"). "Jack the Ripper" was one of the tunes Wray made famous. This particular recipe uses jenever, a personal twist added by Tess Posthumus, owner of the bars Flying Dutchmen Cocktails and Dutch Courage in Amsterdam. There will be more from her later. I'm leaving the directions in metric units because they're very precise and there are too many weird fractions when I convert.

50 milliliters dry vermouth

40 milliliters Bobby's Jenever (or another young-style jenever)

10 milliliters Grand Marnier

Lemon peel (for garnish)

Add vermouth, jenever, and Grand Marnier to a cocktail shaker. Shake and strain into a coupe glass. Garnish with a lemon peel.

Synthpop, Post-Punk & "Darkwave" (And Any Other Labels That May Have Been Retroactively Applied to the Umbrella Genre We Just Used to Call "New Wave")

Even though there's a massive number of great bands from the US and the rest of the world that would comfortably fit in this category, my brain draws an immediate association with England, as that's where these genres' most iconic performers originated. I'm talking the very obvious ones like Depeche Mode (Basildon), The Cure (Blackpool), the Smiths (Manchester), Joy Division/New Order (also Manchester), and Echo & the Bunnymen (Liverpool). And nothing, to me, says "classic English-ness" more than gin and cask ale.

BASIL SMASH

Serves: 1

There are millions of gin cocktails I could have used here (and there will be more to come later in this book) but in honor of the greatest synthpop band in history's home district—that would be Basildon, birthplace of Depeche Mode, who provided the soundtrack for my introverted (and needlessly tortured) teen years—we're going to go with a modern classic that's all about the basil. This particular version comes from Downton Distillery (no relation to the fictional Abbey, and the owners are tired of people making that comment) in Downton, Wiltshire. The distillery's Explorer's Gin is a real banger, with offbeat botanicals like Western red cedar, Brazilian pink pepper, and Szechuan pepper.

Lots of fresh basil (the more the merrier)

1 ounce lemon juice

$\frac{1}{2}$ ounce simple syrup or 1 teaspoon sugar

$1\frac{2}{3}$ ounces Explorer's Gin (or similar)

Ice cubes (enough to fill the glass)

Muddle the basil leaves, lemon juice, and simple syrup in a cocktail shaker. Add the gin and lots of ice to the shaker and shake very hard—make like The Damned and "smash it up!" Fill a rocks or Old Fashioned glass with ice and strain the contents of the shaker into the glass.

Traditional English Ales

- Fuller's London Porter

The absolute gold standard of porters, bar none.

- Timothy Taylor's Landlord

No, it's not the tool man from *Home Improvement*, it's the quintessential English pale ale.

- Greene King Abbot Ale

If you're noticing a pattern here, you're right. I'm trying to highlight prime examples of particular English styles and this one ticks that box for the Extra Special Bitter category. The malt really shines here, as do some fruity notes from the yeast, so expect some nuttiness and a bit of raisin-esque character.

- Samuel Smith's Oatmeal Stout

I'm going to cheat a little bit here and include a non-cask, non- "Real Ale" among my suggestions. Even though the Samuel Smith Brewery owns some of the oldest pubs in all of Great Britain—including the iconic Ye Olde Cheshire Cheese, whose origins can be traced back to the time of the Great Fire of London—its offerings are decidedly modern draft (and bottles, of course). Sam's silky Oatmeal Stout is on so many British beer aficionados' short lists, it would be a crime not to include it.

Punk/Hardcore

Punk (and subgenres like Hardcore), in all of its DIY, "fuck authority" glory, is best enjoyed with beverages that reflect that scrappy, unpretentious ethos. No complicated mixology here. A Boilermaker (a shot of whiskey and a beer) is as fancy as things should get. You want something that's going to evoke the sort of (unironic, hipster-free) dank dive bars that gave birth to the scene. The good news is that since you're staying home, you don't have to be skeeved out by bathrooms that make you want to get a tetanus shot after you've had to use them.

If you were in one of those establishments, you'd likely get a blank, judgmental stare if you tried to order a Manhattan. And the craftiest draught or bottle you'd be likely to find, on a good day, would be something like Yuengling Lager. But most times you'd be lucky get a Pabst Blue Ribbon, and you'd be grateful for that!

Boilermakers (a.k.a. a Shot and a Beer)

No-bullshit simplicity may be the name of the game, but so is nonconformity and a desire to stick it to "the man." So instead of just a Bud Light or Miller High Life served alongside a shot of Jameson, get a little creative here. (By the way, some use the term boilermaker to refer to the drink when you actually pour the shot into the beer. I use it to mean "shot and a beer," side by side.) Try these combos:

• Blanton's Single Barrel Bourbon and Great Lakes Edmund Fitzgerald Porter

Normally I would advocate drinking Blanton's neat without any accompaniment (don't you dare put it in an Old Fashioned!), but a boilermaker isn't technically a cocktail, it's just two beverages that you drink side by side. The pronounced vanilla, maple, and caramel notes perfectly complement the chocolatey, coffee-like roasty-ness of a porter. And since bourbon is as American as spirits get, let's keep the pairing firmly in the USA. Edmund Fitzgerald, from Cleveland's Great Lakes Brewing Co., has been one of the best of the bunch for decades.

• Catoctin Creek Roundstone Rye and Allagash White

I call this the Spice Duo (think of it as the nineties British pop sensation's reunion if three of them sit it out). The pairing offers two kinds of spicy sensations: the peppery notes of Virginia distillery Catoctin Creek's rye whiskey and the coriander of the Belgian-style witbier. As far as American versions of wits go, Allagash is venerable and peerless.

• Westward American Single Malt Whiskey and Breakside Pilsner

Portland, Oregon, has a pretty punk rock attitude, so here's a pairing of one of the best whiskeys and best interpretations of a classic pils, both produced in the Rose City.

- One Eight District Made Bourbon and Right Proper Senate Beer

Washington, D.C. is considered the birthplace of hardcore—if you disagree, Bad Brains and Ian MacKaye would like to have a word with you. One Eight Distilling is one of the many amazing distilleries in the District and Right Proper is the best brewery to come out of the nation's capital in a long time. Senate employs the recipe used by D.C.'s long-defunct nineteenth and early twentieth-century brewery Chr. Heurich Brewery for the pre-Prohibition beer of the same name.

Industrial

This may seem like a way-too-niche genre to include in this space, but industrial has been a major part of my world since the late eighties (and if you don't like it, go write your own book!). For this one, I consulted my old friend, Kevin Snell of the band Chmcl Str8jckt (on Cleopatra Records), and asked him what he's drinking when listening to artists of his ilk. He didn't even have to think about it: "Bourbon. Neat." And, since there are few locations that are as connected to the industrial scene than Chicago—home of Wax Trax! Records and birthplace of Ministry—I'm going to shine the spotlight on some Windy City whiskeys.

- FEW Bourbon: Founded in 2011 in the Chicagoland college town of Evanston, Illinois—the college being Northwestern University, of course—FEW Spirits has quickly achieved "iconic" status, air that is certainly rarefied within the realm of craft booze. This should be the first bourbon you reach for when you spin those LPs filled with aggressive electronic music. (By the way, if you're looking for something to pair with Grunge, look no further than FEW's All Secrets Known, a bourbon produced in collaboration with Alice in Chains).

- Koval Single Barrel Bourbon: Based in Chicago proper since 2008, Koval offers an eclectic array of spirits that hit many of the major categories—brandy, gin, liqueur, and, of course, whiskey. One of the things that sets the distillery's bourbon apart is its mash bill: It has the requisite 51 percent corn—the bare minimum—to qualify as bourbon, while the remaining 49 percent comes from millet.

I'm going to bend the rules a bit and suggest one more whiskey, this time from Canada, and definitely not bourbon because a distillery can't call it "bourbon" unless it's produced in the United States. One of my absolute favorite industrial bands is Skinny Puppy and they're from Vancouver originally. So, in SP's honor, I want to make one recommendation from a British Columbia-based distillery.

As far as the entire drinking world is concerned, there's no greater authority on Canadian spirits than Davin de Kergommeaux, author of *Canadian Whisky: The Portable Expert* and coauthor, with Blair Phillips, of *The Definitive Guide to Canadian Distilleries*.

"Easy," he said. "Shelter Point is number one."

That would be Shelter Point Farm & Distillery in Oyster River, B.C., on the eastern coast of Vancouver Island. Its whisky (remember, no "e," since this is Canada) features a 100 percent malted and unmalted barley base, produced on a custom-designed copper pot still.

Tied for number two, in de Kergommeaux's expert opinion, are Lohin McKinnon Single Malt from Central City Brewers & Distillers in Surrey and Commodore Canadian Single Malt from Odd Society Spirits in Vancouver. If you want to spice things up—literally—try Odd Society's Prospector Canadian Rye Whisky, made from 100 percent Northern British Columbia Rye and aged in charred new American white oak barrels.

Jazz

The classy, classic American genre demands classy, classic cocktails. And which of those cocktails really depends on which kind of jazz we're talking about. If it's New Orleans–style, it goes without saying you're going to want to drink something that goes down (Big) Easy. And that may not be as simple as it sounds because the choices are endless. After all, New Orleans is the reputed birthplace of the American cocktail. The drink that's come to be known as the Old Fashioned reportedly originated there. But since this book is going to include more than a few different riffs on that iconic beverage, let's opt, instead, for a Sazerac.

SAZERAC

Serves: 1

Ice cubes (to chill the glass)

¼ ounce absinthe (to rinse)

1 sugar cube or ½ teaspoon sugar

3 dashes Peychaud's Bitters[*]

2 ounces rye whiskey or cognac[**]

Lemon peel (for garnish)

Before you start playing around with ingredients, chill a rocks or Old Fashioned glass (best way to do this is by filling it with ice). Once it's chilled, discard the ice and rinse the glass with absinthe. Put this glass aside. In a separate glass (solely for mixing), add in the sugar and bitters, then crush/combine the sugar with the bitters and add in the whiskey or cognac. Strain the whiskey/bitters/sugar mix into the first absinthe-rinsed glass and garnish with a lemon peel.

---

[*]   Usually, I'm pretty agnostic about specific brands, but Peychaud's is inextricably linked with New Orleans. It was created in the city nearly two centuries ago by a Creole apothecary named Antoine Amédée Peychaud.

[**]   Cognac very likely may have been the original spirit base for the cocktail, as it was widely consumed—especially in New Orleans—in the early nineteenth century, before the Great French Wine Blight of the mid-1800s made anything grape-based hard to come by (and cognac, a brandy, is essentially wine that's been distilled and aged). Whiskey—very likely rye whiskey and then bourbon—started replacing cognac in cocktails.

When I think of jazz in general, I think of the Jazz Age (even though many of the greats—Coltrane, Bird, et al—emerged a decade or two later). When I think Jazz Age, I think Prohibition, which usually leads my brain to bathtub gin. But for our purposes, let's forget the bathtub and spin some Duke Ellington or Billie Holliday and get back to basics with the great gin-based recipes that were popular during the Noble Experiment and in the years following Repeal. Since we already visited with some UK distilleries, we're going to keep things firmly US-based. (I mean, why not? We were the ones dumb enough to ban alcohol for fourteen years.)

GIN RICKEY

Serves: 1

Even though its origins predate the era by at least twenty years, the Gin Rickey gets a shout-out in that quintessential work of Jazz Age fiction, The Great Gatsby. And that's good enough for me.

2 ounces gin

Juice of 1 lime

Club soda

Lime wheel (for garnish)

Load up a tall, highball-style glass with ice. Pour in the gin and lime juice and top off with club soda. Garnish with two or three lime wheels. Almost too easy (honestly, the best mixed drinks are). No need to overcomplicate things.

As jazz and big band evolve through the forties, fifties, and sixties, music and drinking become almost synonymous with the Rat Pack. And there are two libations I immediately associate with Sinatra and his gang. The first doesn't come close to qualifying as a cocktail: it's Jack Daniel's and a splash of water on the rocks. If you're a purist, that's perfectly fine, but if you're interested in exploring some other Tennessee Whiskeys, might I suggest Uncle Nearest 1856 Premium Whiskey—named for the first African American master distiller, Nathaniel "Nearest" Green, the man who actually taught Jack Daniel how to distill. Fawn Weaver, cofounder of the Nearest Green Foundation, launched the whiskey for modern consumers in 2017.

As for martinis, just do me a favor and forget the vodka. I'm never *not* going to think of it as a gin drink. (Fight me!) And I like my martinis dirty, and hopefully you do, too. If not, just forgo the brine.

DIRTY GIN MARTINI

Serves: 1

3 ounces London dry-style gin*
$\frac{1}{2}$ ounce olive brine
$\frac{1}{2}$ ounce dry vermouth
3 olives on a skewer (for garnish)

Fill a cocktail shaker with ice and pour in gin, brine, and vermouth. Stir (never shake . . . I'm looking at you, 007!) and strain into a martini glass. Garnish with olives on a skewer. And you'd better not waste those olives when you're done. If you're not going to eat them, let me have them!

---

*   There are so many to choose from in this day and age, but I'm going to go with something like the Freeland Dry Gin out of Portland, Oregon (Navy strength, at 114 proof, so you might want to dial it down to $2\frac{1}{2}$ ounces), Conniption American Dry Gin from Durham Distillery in Durham, North Carolina, or 3 Floyds Distilling's Oude Boatface Not Normal London Dry Gin from Munster, Indiana.

Reggae

You might think I'm going to recommend some sweet, tropical-fruit-forward cocktail because it evokes the Caribbean. That's where you'd be wrong.

When I think Jamaica (and its enduring musical traditions), I think Wray & Ting, a simple combination of Wray & Nephew overproof white rum—the stuff is ubiquitous across the island nation—and the refreshing Caribbean grapefruit soda, Ting. That's it.

If you can't find Wray & Nephew, any Jamaican overproof, unaged rum will suffice. You should be able to locate Ting (or another sweetened grapefruit-flavored soft drink) at an ethnic grocery store, but if you can't, you have a couple of options to try to replicate it. If you like making things difficult, squeeze some juice out of a fresh grapefruit (or two) and mix it with plain seltzer and a tablespoon of agave syrup. That's about as healthy a grapefruit-flavored soft drink as you're going to get. A somewhat easier method would be to just add the agave to grapefruit-flavored seltzer (it's actually pretty hard to avoid at most supermarkets, as grapefruit is among the most popular flavors).

WRAY & TING

Serves: 1

Ice (enough to fill the glass)

2 ounces Wray & Nephew overproof white rum (or similar)

6 ounces Ting grapefruit soda (or equivalent/homemade
alternative)

Fill a tall, highball-style glass with ice. Pour in the rum and then the soda. Give it a quick stir. Enjoy a whole new plane of refreshment!

JAMAICAN RUM OLD FASHIONED

Serves: 1

If you're looking for something fancier, I recommend having this rum-soaked riff on a traditionally whiskey-based drink.

- 1 sugar cube or ½ teaspoon sugar
- 3–4 dashes bitters (Angostura will be easiest to find, but there are plenty of small, artisanal options as well)
- 1 teaspoon water
- 1 giant ice cube/sphere or 2–3 smaller ice cubes
- 2 ounces aged Jamaican Rum (Appleton Estate 8 Year Reserve Rum is a good option)
- Orange peel (for garnish)

Add the sugar, bitters, and water—in that order—to a rocks-style glass and stir together until the sugar dissolves. Add in the ice cube(s)/sphere. Pour in the rum and lightly stir contents together. Rub the orange peel around the rim of glass before giving it one final twist and dropping it in the glass as a garnish.

Country

Sorry, I'm just not a fan of this genre, so you won't get any recommendations from me here. Besides, is there anything sadder than sitting at home and drinking alone to country music? Let's talk TV now. Okay, more likely streaming, but I'm never going to stop calling it TV!

Cobra Kai

When it debuted on YouTube's short-lived, premium original-content Red platform, the nostalgia-soaked *Karate Kid* reboot series scored some twenty-million views in its first weekend, which almost crashed the server. And when Netflix picked it up two seasons later it became the number-one streaming series at the time, practically achieving *Stranger Things*-like numbers. So, it's safe to assume that some of you are probably watching it. Speaking of season 3, one of the biggest highlights occurred when Daniel LaRusso returned to Okinawa for the first time since he first visited with Mr. Miyagi in *The Karate Kid Part II*. During Daniel-san's reunion with his love interest from that film, Kumiko, there's a great close-up shot of breaking ice that calls back to the scene in the 1986 movie when Daniel wins a bet by Karate-chopping through several frozen blocks at once. When the shot goes wider, though, we discover that he and Kumiko are actually in some bougie bar in the now-dramatically-Westernized village from "KKP2," drinking a clear liquid on the rocks. I would bet my house on my assumption that said liquid is Awamori, the native spirit of Okinawa.

It's similar to shōchū produced on Japan's main islands—it's also made with koji—but the fermentable base is exclusively long-grain indica rice, which made its way to the island by way of Thailand. It also tends to have a higher alcohol content than shōchū—roughly in the low thirties, versus around 25 percent ABV for most shōchū. (See the side box, Shōchū & Awamori, for more details).

This is just a very convoluted way of saying that you should be drinking Awamori when you're bingeing a season or two of *Cobra Kai*. Rocks is the way to go, in my humble opinion, but the spirit is quite versatile in cocktails as well.

SHŌCHŪ & AWAMORI

I could go on forever about them, but you've got to get to the rest of this book, so I'll keep it short. The basics: Shōchū—not to be in any way confused with Korea's soju—can be distilled from any one of fifty-odd substrates, but the most common varieties are made from sweet potato (imo), barley (mugi), rice (kome) and buckwheat (soba). Another of the major styles is kokuto, made from a type of sugar often called "black sugar" and originated on the Amami Islands (part of the Kagoshima Prefecture). There's a bit of regionality with the other four as well, as they're all relatively synonymous with specific prefectures in Kyushu, the southwestern-most of the Japanese archipelago's main islands. Shōchū can be produced throughout Japan, but the vast majority (somewhere in the neighborhood of 90 percent) is native to Kyushu.

Awamori, on the other hand, is made exclusively in Okinawa and distilled from long-grain indica rice—versus japonica rice, whose grains tend to be shorter and rounder and form the basis for kome shōchū as well as saké.

Shōchū's ABV typically is around 25 percent, but there are varieties available that hover around 40 percent—those often are made to appeal to Western consumers who don't always associate anything with a sub-30 percent ABV with a spirit. A couple of American producers make shōchū—specifically American Shōchū Company in Frederick Maryland and, to a lesser extent, St. George Spirits in Alameda, California (known more for its American single malt whiskey and its gins). The former's barley-based Umai! Shōchū is 24 percent ABV and, therefore, more in line with the strength of most Japanese shōchū (again, with plenty of exceptions). But the small Maryland distiller also makes the 40 percent ABV Roy's Demon, which it dubs "the whiskey lover's shōchū." St. George's California Shōchū is also 40 percent ABV, but it's distilled from the Golden State's version of saké rice, Calrose.

One more thing you need to know about shōchū and Awamori, before I get too deep into the weeds about them. A great deal of their flavor and aroma come from koji, a type of mold that helps kickstart fermentation by releasing the enzymes that break down starches into fermentable sugars (beer and whiskey achieve that by malting the grain, and brandies already have the fermentable sugars present in their fruits, so no additional step is necessary). Koji also performs the same task in saké (as well as soy sauce) and is responsible for much of that beverage's character as well.

Awamori Cocktails

Traditional collides with modern in these drinks created by an international roster of bartenders, using the Awamori brand Ryukyu 1429.

HEALING HIGHBALL

Serves: 1

This one is the brainchild of Giulio Amodio, the bar manager of China Tang at the Dorchester Hotel in London. You'll have to get your hands on some aloe vera juice (OKF Aloe Vera King is a popular Korean brand), which you should be able to easily find in an Asian grocery store or Whole Foods.

Clear chunk ice (enough to fill glass)
$1^2/_3$ ounces Ryukyu 1429 Kaze 5-year aged Awamori
Aloe vera soda* (to top off)

Fill a highball glass with clear chunk ice. Add the Awamori and top off with the aloe vera soda.

---

* To make aloe vera soda, combine 20 ounces aloe vera drink (such as Aloe Vera King) with $2^1/_2$ ounces sauvignon blanc and 1 ounce citric acid.

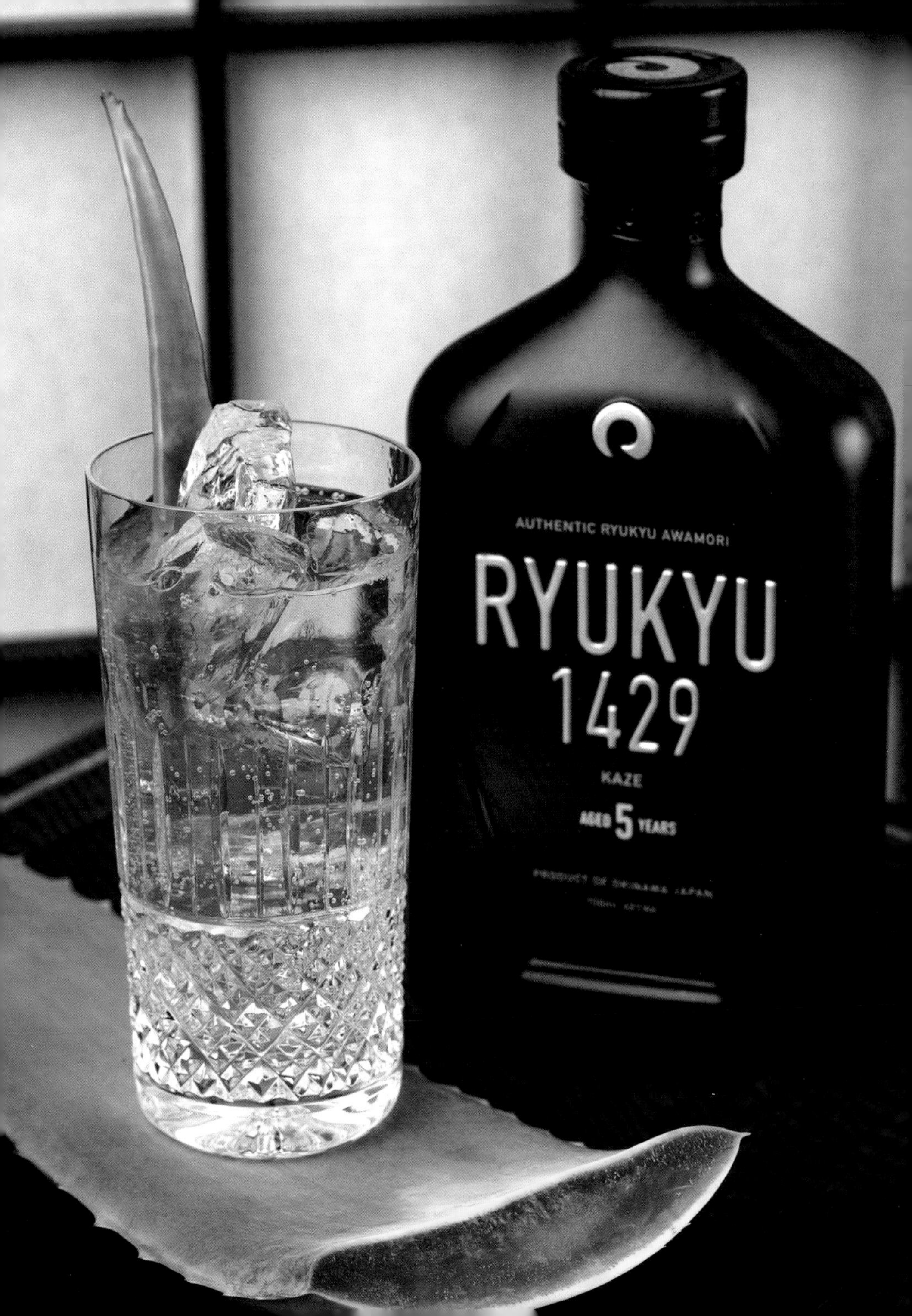
AUTHENTIC RYUKYU AWAMORI
RYUKYU
1429
KAZE
AGED 5 YEARS

IBING FOR INTROVERTS

STIR FRY HIGHBALL

Serves: 1

Here's another highball of sorts, this one created by Joe Churchill of Amsterdam's The Stockroom.

1½ ounces Ryukyu 1429 Awamori Mizu (or similar Awamori)

½ ounce yuzu-infused Ginjo saké (like Akashi-Tai Ginjo Yuzushu)

1²/₃ tablespoons spring onion shrub*

1½ teaspoons citric acid

¼ teaspoon Japanese shiso bitters

Fever-Tree tonic water (to top off)

Honeycomb folded in rice paper (for garnish)

Throw all ingredients together in a cocktail shaker. Pour into a Collins highball glass, top off with tonic water, and garnish with a honeycomb folded in rice paper.

---

*   For the spring onion shrub, combine 320 milliliters water with 180 grams spring onion whites (discard green tails) and 500 grams pure honey and simmer in a saucepan for 8½ minutes. Let cool with spring onions still in the mixture, then strain and fortify with 45 milliliters rice vinegar.

WOKOU GIMLET

Serves: 2

If you ever wanted a drink that says "Okinawa, by way of Iceland," this is your jam. Kristjan Bjarni Johannson, head bartender at Reykjavik's KOL, crafted this situation.

$1^2/_3$ ounces coconut washed Rykyu 1429 Tsuchi Awamori

$^1/_3$ ounce grapefruit juice

5 teaspoons yuzu/grape/lemon cordial*

1 barspoon lime juice

Ice (enough to fill the glasses)

Nikka whiskey or other malt whiskey (to spray over the final product)

Shiso leaves, dried limes, and honeycombs wrapped in rice paper**
   (for garnish)

In a cocktail shaker, combine all ingredients. Fill two Collins highball glasses with ice and shake and double strain the contents of the shaker into the glasses. Spray malt whiskey over the final products. Garnish with shiso leaves, dried limes, and honeycombs wrapped in rice paper.

---

* To make the cordial, grind grapefruit zest into 1,000 milliliters sugar and rub it in. Add 600 milliliters lemon juice, 300 milliliters grapefruit juice, and 150 milliliters yuzu juice. When the sugar is dissolved, strain the zest from the mixture.

** This garnish may not always be the easiest thing to find, so sliced yuzu or lemon would suffice if you don't want your drinks to look naked. However, honeycomb candy (see the side box, Honeycomb Candy, for more details) also makes for an attractive garnish.

HONEYCOMB CANDY

1 cup granulated sugar
1$\frac{1}{4}$ ounces honey
1$\frac{3}{4}$ ounces glucose powder
$\frac{1}{4}$ cup water
$\frac{1}{2}$ ounce baking soda

Combine the sugar, honey, glucose powder, and water in a large pan, stir, and cook on medium-high heat until a light amber caramel is formed. Then, remove from heat, add in the baking soda, stir for about a minute, and pour onto a baking tray. Once cool, break honeycomb apart into bite-sized, garnish-friendly pieces. It seems a long way to go for a garnish, but you can use the rest of it on ice creams, cakes, and whatever else might activate the ol' sweet tooth.

CODA

Serves: 1

A pair of American expats living in Japan, Stephen Lyman and Christopher Pellegrini, are the preeminent Western authorities on shōchū. They joined forces to launch Honkaku Spirits, which brings rare finds among Japanese spirits to American audiences. They offered this simple recipe to demonstrate the spirit's versatility.

No, this isn't a salute to the famous compilation album by Led Zeppelin. It's a portmanteau of "coffee" and "soda." Simple as that. And it's also extremely low-ABV so this is good if you're taking it easy.

Ice (enough to fill the glass)

3 ounces coffee (all the cool kids seem to be drinking cold brew these days)

3 ounces club soda

½ ounce Mugi Hokka roasted barley shōchū (or other barley-based shōchū)

In an ice-filled rocks glass, add coffee, club soda, and shōchū. Do a very mild stir to avoid releasing the carbonation.

Stranger Things

Since I name-checked *Stranger Things*, I can't not include something to drink that's drowning in as much eighties nostalgia as the streaming era's first bona fide blockbuster. And, no, I'm not going to recommend wine coolers. What I am going to offer is a slightly more modern, boozier twist on an extremely polarizing fruit-forward Reagan-era beverage, the Fuzzy Navel. I'm going to go out on a limb and say that New Jersey-based bartender, magazine publisher, and author Ray Foley was ahead of his time when he christened this concoction. (I was lucky enough to be on a press trip in Curaçao with him in 2005 and he is the embodiment of a ball-busting bon vivant. I was grateful for that because I was the shy, reserved, relatively inexperienced one among a handful of veritable industry celebrities, so I was glad there was someone else doing most of the talking). The brands available to him at the time were limited and he still managed to create something that's nothing short of iconic (for better or worse). The original recipe calls for equal parts orange juice and peach "schnapps"—again, not "schnaps" in the true sense, just an artificially flavored peach liqueur. I keep the OJ—squeeze your own if you really want to be fancy—but go craft on the liqueur. Two Georgia-based producers (of course), Savannah's Ghost Coast Distillery and Roswell's Blended Family Spirits, offer some great options. What's more, I'm going to add some true peach schnaps—one "p"—and by that, I mean actual, non-sweet brandy distilled from peaches. It gives it more of a kick, while staying true to its orchard roots.

JEFF'S
FUZZIER NAVEL

Serves: 1

Ice (enough to fill the glass)

3 ounces fresh-squeezed orange juice

3 ounces Blended Family or Ghost Coast Peach Liqueur

1 ounce peach brandy (Purcellville, Virginia's Catoctin Creek and
   Charleston, South Carolina's High Wire Distilling make great
   ones, though availability is limited. You can also find some
   alternatives from schnaps-producing regions like Germany's
   Black Forest and Austria)

Peach/orange slice (for garnish)

Fill a tall, highball or Collins-style glass with ice. Pour in all ingredients
and stir a few times. Garnish with the peach or orange slice.

The Marvelous Mrs. Maisel & Mad Men

I know, I know, they're completely different series, but they're set in the relatively same era (give or take a few years—season 3 and beyond of *Maisel* overlaps the time frame of the first few seasons of *Mad Men*) and in the same city.

I feel like suggesting an Old Fashioned or a Manhattan here would be a little too on-the-nose (not to mention lazy on my part), and I want to avoid a mint julep here because it evokes the "My Old Kentucky Home" Derby-Day episode from *Mad Men* season 3—the one where Roger Sterling makes the viewing audience very uncomfortable when he sings the song from which the episode takes its name in squirm-inducing blackface.

Instead, let's go with a couple of simple, two-to-three-minute gin drinks that were pervasive across New York watering holes in the late fifties and early sixties.

GIMLET

Serves: 1

Ice (for the shaker)

3 ounces gin

Juice of 1 lime

½ ounce simple syrup

Lime wheel (for garnish)

In a cocktail shaker, combine ice with gin, lime juice, and simple syrup. Shake and strain into a rocks or coupe glass, depending on how fancy you're feeling. Garnish with a lime wheel.

TOM COLLINS

Serves: 1

If lemon is your citrus of choice and you're into fizzy refreshment, then the Collins is the classic for you.

Ice (for the shaker and the glass)

2 ounces gin

1 ounce lemon juice

½ ounce simple syrup

Club soda (to top off)

Maraschino or Luxardo cherry skewered through a lemon wheel
(for garnish)

In a cocktail shaker, combine ice with gin, lemon juice, and simple syrup. Shake vigorously until it feels like your hand is going to get frostbite. Strain into a tall, Collins- or highball-style glass filled with ice. Top off with club soda and give the drink a couple of light stirs with a barspoon. Garnish with a maraschino or Luxardo cherry skewered through a lemon wheel.

SNAPPY AF RED SNAPPER

(A.K.A. A BLOODY MARY WITH GIN)

Serves: 1

The characters on both shows were very frequently nursing hangovers and, as far as hairs of the dog go, nothing beats a Bloody Mary. However, we're going to bend the rules a little because, as I mentioned earlier, I've almost exclusively been using gin in place of vodka in my bloodies for several years now. And that changes the name of the drink to the Red Snapper (hey, I don't make the rules). I've also been experimenting a bunch with Dutch jenever, gin's ancestor, which takes this tomatoey brunch staple to a whole new dimension.

6 ounces San Marzano tomato juice (not cheap or easy, but you'll thank me)

7 pepper mill turns of fresh black pepper, or ¼ teaspoon pre-ground pepper

4–5 shakes celery salt

Juice of 1 lime

Ice (for the shaker and the glass)

3 ounces gin (go big or go home—oh, wait, you're already there)

1 teaspoon hot sauce

4–5 dashes Worcestershire sauce

Celery stalk (of course), cheddar cheese cube, 3 Castelvetrano olives, cornichon, peppadew, lime wedge (for garnish)

(continued)

Crush the San Marzano tomatoes in a blender or food processor. They're typically going to come in a 28-ounce can—make sure the can says "D.O.P." on it and has a serial number stamped on it, otherwise you're getting scammed—so you can get a few drinks out of the resulting juice. Rim a large glass (shaker pint is ideal) with the pepper and celery salt. A rub of a lime wedge around the rim before applying might get the pepper and salt to stick better. Fill half of that glass with ice. Shake all of the ingredients in a cocktail shaker with ice and strain into the glass. Drop in the celery stalk, skewer the remaining garnishes together (this might require a couple of skewers), and place on the glass. If there's any of the drink left in the shaker, save it for the next pour.

A MISFIT'S MICHELADA

Serves: 2

If you don't have any gin on hand, or if you're keen on something beer-based with a Mexican influence, you can jazz up a classic michelada.

½ teaspoon salt

1 teaspoon Tajín seasoning or chili powder

¼ cup fresh lime juice (save some wedges for garnish)

Ice (enough to fill the glasses)

1 (12-ounce) pilsner or helles lager (Traditionally, you'd go with a Dos Equis, Corona, Tecate, Sol, or Modelo Especial. But if you want to mix it up a bit, why not try something like Great Lakes Mexican Lager with Lime or Stone Buenaveza Salt and Lime Lager?)

12 ounces Clamato or tomato juice (As I noted in my bloody mary recipe, I like to get fancy by throwing some San Marzano tomatoes into the blender)

2 teaspoons Worcestershire sauce

1 teaspoon soy sauce

½ ounce hot sauce (Cholula is perfect here)

(continued on page 46)

½ ounce pickle brine

2 large sour pickles and 2 pickled jalapeños or 12 sliced jalapeño
    rings, divided (for garnish)

Mix the salt and Tajin or chili powder in a small bowl, then spread
it out on a piece of wax paper or very flat plate. Rub a lime wedge
around the rims of two glasses (pint glasses or large goblets should
work). Roll the rims of the glasses in the spice mixture, then fill both
glasses with ice. Put all of the other ingredients into a cocktail shaker
or bowl and gently stir (you don't want to agitate the carbonation).
Divide evenly into the glasses and garnish each glass with a pickle (on
a skewer or standing upright in the glass), a whole pickled jalapeño or
6 rings on a skewer, and a lime wedge.

Parks & Recreation

The only right answer here is to always have a bottle of Lagavulin Scotch whiskey on hand. The eight-year-old won't break the bank. The sixteen-year-old will probably cost you around $120 or $130. Ron Swanson famously acquired a majority stake in the distillery toward the end of the show's run. In reality, Diageo owns it, but the global spirits giant has made Swanson— well, Nick Offerman—a brand ambassador of sorts. In 2021, Lagavulin released a special Nick Offerman label for an eleven-year-old single malt finished in casks that previously held Guinness stout. The bottling honored Offerman's dad on Father's Day.

The Handmaid's Tale

The Elisabeth Moss-fronted Hulu series is just as upsetting and stressful as the Margaret Atwood source material. Just drink straight from whatever bottle is in reach when you're watching it.

PART II

TIME TO VENTURE OUT

You can't stay home all the time, but you also don't have to have all of your energy drained going out. Here's how to make the most out of being out and about in the world.

MIX, DON'T MINGLE

(PLAYING IT COOL IN A
CRAFT COCKTAIL BAR)

I have a confession to make: I truly believe that bartenders got it right the first time, way back in the early nineteenth century, when they invented the drink that came to be known as the Old Fashioned. In my arrogant opinion, there never needed to be another cocktail.

Yet, here we are, in a new cocktail golden age, one that is a worldwide phenomenon encompassing every continent (yes, even Antarctica. The scientists there have to drink too, you know!). Bartenders have, like chefs, become celebrities. And rightly so because they're just as creative and just as attuned to what satisfies the palates of their devoted fan bases.

But when I'm in a so-called craft cocktail bar and I don't see an Old Fashioned on the drink menu, I'm going to order one anyway. (Every bartender knows how to make one.)

It's almost like a reconnaissance mission for me. It's the baseline—the cocktail against which all other cocktails will be measured. If their Old Fashioned is shit, I'm probably not going to like anything else they make. If it's sublime—and more often than not in the right bar, it is—then I'm going to be pretty okay with them making me whatever cocktail(s) made them famous (well, at least locally). And that may sound as though I'm just being an asshole and

testing them like some kind of secret shopper. But honestly, I'm really just testing myself. Let me explain with what may seem like a tooting-my-own-horn kind of plug.

My first book was called *The Year of Drinking Adventurously: 52 Ways to Get Out of Your Comfort Zone.* It may seem like I was telling *readers* what to drink to get out of their comfort zones, but secretly I was telling *myself* to get out of my own comfort zone. I'm picky and I'm cranky and often need to be nudged beyond "my usual"—at least as far as booze is concerned. And an exquisitely crafted Old Fashioned is going to loosen me up just enough to enable that to happen.

I'll usually know which way my evening is going after the first sip. When it's going to go well, this is the point at which I start scouring the drinks menu, scanning the ingredients in each of the proprietary house cocktails on offer. There are certain spirits I just can't stand. (Just because I'm willing to try new things, doesn't mean I've stopped being picky.)

If you're anything like me in this regard, I behoove you to find a space at the bar. I love a quiet, corner two-top (with an empty chair across from me) as much as the next introvert, but in these sorts of bars I'm actually going to want to engage another human being.

Now, don't get excited or shudder too loudly. My interaction will be limited to the person behind the bar and only if it's not a particularly busy night. (I wouldn't recommend trying this between Thursday and Saturday, unless it's when the bar just opens at around 4 p.m.)

It's never going to be a steady conversation. (This isn't going to be the old TV/movie trope of bartender-as-therapist.) There's still plenty of time to retreat into your phone, book, or own world. But intermittently you'll be building a rapport with the one person who will truly take care of you during your solo outing. The best bartenders are, at their heart, booze nerds and they are more than eager to geek out with you (time permitting, between pours).

You might even get to be a guinea pig for some new recipes that they're workshopping that aren't on the menu or that they're planning on entering into cocktail competitions (it's like getting to see the work print of an independent film before it hits the festival circuit).

If you're really lucky (and the bartender genuinely likes you), you could find yourself sipping a neat pour of something from their secret stash, a spirit or liqueur that's not available to most other guests and usually out of the bar patrons' eyeshot.

Case in point number one: On Christmas Eve, 2014, I brought my laptop to a bar formerly known as Jackson 20 in the hotel formerly known as the Monaco in Alexandria, Virginia. (Monaco owner Kimpton sold the property to Marriott, which renamed it the Alexandrian. The bar inside is now called King and Rye.) I was about seven weeks away from my publisher's deadline for *The Year of Drinking Adventurously* and had to pound out about one thousand words that day before I could enjoy eggnog with the in-laws. Typing away on a MacBook Pro on a barstool surrounded by traveling revelers will always pique the interest of the barkeep. We got to talking and eventually he alerted me to a bottle of Pappy van Winkle he was hiding under the bar. God bless us, everyone!

Case in point number two: In one of my handful of homes away from home, Amsterdam's Rosalia's Menagerie, former head bartender Wouter Bosch once let me sip a shot from a more than fifty-year-old bottle of Italy's legendary artichoke liqueur, Cynar.

I wouldn't be relaying these stories if I didn't remember them. A geeky conversation with a bartender creates imbibing experiences that one never forgets. And neither of these moments would have occurred if I had been with a group of people.

New York State of Mind

New York City was way ahead of the curve with its craft cocktail scene, thanks to a collection of institutions that have since made their owners, beverage directors, and bartenders famous. The first few venues that immediately come to mind are Death & Co., Dead Rabbit, Please Don't Tell (PDT), Mace, and Brooklyn's Clover Club. Mace is particularly notable because it's responsible for launching "Miracle" holiday pop-up bars that now take over venues across the US and many parts of the world from Thanksgiving week through Christmas. (I'm an enormous Christmas fan and I look forward to these each year because I can quietly soak in the season through the magical décor and spiced drinks.) It all started at Miracle on 9th Street at Mace before it expanded exponentially. There are far too many more to name in at least four of the five boroughs, not to mention across the Hudson in Hoboken and Jersey City (though I will give a shout-out to the Archer in the latter).

But when it comes to New York, these days I'm seeking out places that offer something different than the classic mixology dens. That's why I've become a fan of Katana Kitten, a cocktail bar in the West Village, that infuses many Japanese elements into its design and its drinks menu. If you like a negroni, you need to try the Megaroni at Katana Kitten: iichiko no saiten shōchū, Rutte Old Simon Jenever, umeshu (Japanese plum-infused spirit), and Caffo Red Bitter. It's a veritable polyglot of a cocktail, speaking Japanese, Dutch, and Italian.

Even though Katana Kitten can get a bit loud and crowded, you're never going to be standing and you're never going to feel self-conscious. It's easy to hide and tune out everyone else, whether at a tiny corner table or on a stool against a small ledge on the wall. You'll forget anyone else is there because you're going to be mainly focused on not just the drinks, but the collection of movie posters from the Japanese releases of mostly Western films, like *Any Which Way You Can* and *The Rocky Horror Picture show*, with the requisite kanji for marketing within Japan. As we get into the international sections later in this book, you'll see why I love museums so much. Katana Kitten is practically a micro-museum of American pop culture, as seen through Japanese eyes. It's a must for film buffs.

The best part is it doesn't try to be a "speakeasy," a concept that seems to have run its course.

New Old Vegas
One exception I'm willing to make regarding that "s" word is Downtown Cocktail Room (DCR) in Las Vegas. Besides, the owners and staff would probably get pissed at me if I called it a speakeasy. Sure, the entrance is something of an enigma. It's down an alley and it's very easy to miss. It's actually the door to two bars: DCR to the left and Mike Morey's Sip 'n' Tip. The door's locked and you'll have to ring the bell (which, I learned, once inside, that it rings to the tune of "Swan Lake.") It takes a minute or two for someone to answer and when they do, they'll ask which bar you want, explaining that DCR is a fancy cocktail bar and Sip 'n' Tip is more of an "industry" place, with draft beers and brighter lighting. It's pretty much the place where the staff of DCR would drink when their shifts are over.

The doorbell is more for crowd control purposes than to sell some sort of under-cover-of-night speakeasy gimmick.

DCR is part of the "new" Vegas Downtown, which is working hard to shake its previously seedy image. It's far from the Strip, so you don't have to deal with that nonsense. Tourists staying on the Strip who venture Downtown tend to stick to the Fremont Street Experience. The subtle signage and the obscure entrance keep the out-of-towners away. My eavesdropping confirmed that locals frequent DCR; I heard a pair of nurses from a nearby hospital venting about the stresses of treating COVID patients.

I was worried that DCR would be too much of a "scene," which turned out to be somewhat true, but it was an acceptable level of "scene-iness" for my taste.

The bonus was that the music wasn't oppressive. I've created a ten-point bar music loudness scale in my head. DCR's playlist alternated between a three and four and briefly spiked to a five. A ten would be "I can't hear myself think, get me the fuck out of here."

And it was a pleasant mix. "Love Cats" by the Cure was playing as I entered the bar which put me in a very positive mood. Then the mix just got intriguingly weird and incongruous, with songs that included Regina Spektor's "Fidelity," "Sex and Candy" by Marcy Playground, and "Falling Skies" by Yungblud featuring Charlotte Lawrence.

Comfy couches give it a lounge vibe and the red glass votive candles throughout induce a mildly meditative state—exactly where a Thinking Introvert wants to be. Some strategically placed red velvet curtains fortified that sense because they evoked *Twin Peaks*.

It's a post-industrial space, so there's a lot of black-painted concrete, including the bar, which is where I made myself comfortable. The friendly bartender, who worked beneath an abstract mural on the bar's back wall, fixed me a Jack Rose. I'm all over anything with an apple brandy base. And DCR's did not disappoint.

Nor did the bar's menu of "noshes," which lets you select two snacks for eight bucks. I chose briny for a nice contrast with the brandy and ate Spanish olives that were almost as big as my palm and—a simple stroke of genius—a gargantuan sour pickle on a stick. The world would be a much happier place if every drink in every bar came with a side of olives and pickles.

Pretention, Be Damned

It must be said: the pretentious air of today's mixology-focused establishments is an absolute turnoff for the introverted. We like to fade into the scenery, we don't want to feel judged because we may not be doing everything "right." An example I frequently cite is a cocktail lounge in Washington, D.C. that shall remain nameless. A friend who owns a booze brand was in town to meet with some of his bar and restaurant accounts and invited me to make a night of it. At the watering hole in question, I ordered what sounded like an unassuming drink. When the server delivered it and I was about to take a sip, he said, "Wait! I have to add the Shalimar." And he commenced to spray my glass with the iconic perfume.

Needless to say, I never went back there again.

Fortunately, there appears to be some backlash toward pretentiousness within the mixology world. There will always be the highfalutin Shalimar-spraying parlors and they will always have their audience. But I'm loving the trend of craft cocktails in casual, no-bullshit settings. It's as though the craft has been infused with a punk rock sensibility and I am 100 percent here for it.

Since I dissed a D.C. bar, I'm going to sing praises of another inside the Beltway. It's the Peoples Drug, right across the Potomac in Alexandria, Virginia. The first big plus: It opens at 11 a.m. (there's food), so day drinking is an option. The name is a nod to Peoples Drug Stores, a chain of drugstores founded in Alexandria, popular in the first half of the twentieth century. It even adopts the aesthetic of a vintage soda-fountain pharmacy, with its neon "Drugs" sign on the wall, shiny tiles, antique lighting, and tin ceiling. It may be a meticulous, artificial recreation of a shop from a bygone era, but it's so laid-back that you'd be forgiven for mistaking it for a greasy spoon. Once you taste the Watermelon Whiskey Smash—Maker's Mark, cold-pressed watermelon juice, mint, lemon, and creole bitters—there's no way to make that mistake again.

JACK ROSE

Serves: 1

It's a classic and Downtown Cocktail Room in Las Vegas reminded me just how amazing it is.

Ice (enough to fill the shaker)

2 ounces apple brandy or applejack (For classic: Laird's Applejack or Laird's Bottled-in-Bond Apple Brandy; A little modern: Copper & Kings Floodwall American Craft Apple Brandy)

1 ounce freshly squeezed lemon juice

½ ounce grenadine

1 dash bitters

Lemon twist

In a cocktail shaker filled with ice, combine the brandy, lemon juice, grenadine, and bitters. Shake aggressively until contents are chilled. Strain into a coupe glass. Squeeze the lemon twist into the drink and rub the twist around the rim.

BLUEBERRY BASIL COOLER

Serves: 1

Here's a fruit of a different color. This refresher is another from Portland-based "mixtresses" Sonia Worcel and Catherine O'Brien.

1 ounce blueberry-basil syrup*

1 1/2 ounces Tanqueray gin

Ice (enough to fill the glass)

2 ounces soda

Juice from 1 lime wedge

Blueberries and basil (for garnish)

Stir syrup and gin together. Serve over ice and top with soda and lime juice. Garnish with blueberries and basil.

---

* To make the blueberry-basil syrup, combine 8 ounces fresh blueberries, 3/4 cup sugar, 3/4 cup water, 2 tablespoons lemon juice, 2 lemon peels from 1 lemon, 20 torn basil leaves, and 1/2 stick cinnamon in a pot on the stove and heat on low until combined. Take cinnamon stick out early (judge by taste). Smash blueberries with a spoon as they soften to release juices. Strain through sieve while hot. Cool and refrigerate.

COFFEE CONUNDRUM

Serves: 1

For a rye-based cocktail that's beyond the norm, here's another one from "mix-tresses" Sonia Worcel and Catherine O'Brien.

2 ounces Bullet rye infused with decaf coffee*

1 ounce Calisaya

½ ounce Lillet

2 dashes Regan's orange bitters

1 large ice cube

Orange peel (for garnish)

Add all ingredients to a cocktail shaker. Stir and strain into a Double Old Fashioned glass over a large ice cube. Garnish with an orange peel.

---

* To make the rye infusion, mix 8 ounces rye with ½ ounce decaf coffee beans and strain after twelve to twenty-four hours (twenty-four hours makes a strong, coffee-forward cocktail)

A DARK, MOODY ESCAPE

(YEP, IT'S TIKI TIME!)

When single people ask me what marriage is like, a response that I wish I'd use more often is "a constant struggle between the forces of light and the forces of darkness." My wife's the former and I'm the latter. And I believe that I'm the good guy in this narrative. She'll often come home to find me sitting with the lights off and the curtains closed, make some snarky comment about me being a Nosferatu-adjacent being, and then aggressively illuminate the house to her visually jarring liking.

I find brightness to be noisy. It stresses me out (well, in addition to most daily occurrences that stress me out). Dimly lit rooms calm me. And that's one of the reasons I find tiki bars so appealing. I'm not talking about the new wave of tiki-adjacent watering holes that attempt to "class up" the concept just so they can charge twenty dollars for a cocktail. You know the places I'm talking about. They've got some palm-frond wallpaper to make the joint look vaguely tropical and all of the bartenders are wearing identical Hawaiian shirts—not the vibrant, funky, early sixties sort, but the bland, muted, light-blue-and-gray kind that George Clooney wore at his law office in *The Descendants*. Oh, and there will be windows. Very large windows with the blinds raised.

Did I mention the music? It's likely to be of the EDM variety because, apparently, the proprietors feel it's just not loud and chaotic enough on its own in there without it.

Check, please! I'm out of here. I'd rather spend my time at the true tiki bars, the ones that understand tiki's origins—the thirties—and celebrate its Golden Age—the fifties and sixties. You know, what everyone's calling "mid-century" now. (When are we going to stop calling it that? I mean, in a couple more decades we're going to be at the middle of a different century and things are going to start to get really confusing!)

Tiki, for me, has always been about the kitsch—the artifice of it all. It's a completely fabricated genre, a hodgepodge of South Seas cultural iconography, poured through a West Coast American filter. I learned just how much that was the case the first time I went to Hawaii in 2015. Sure, there were a couple of tiki bars in Waikiki, but they adopted their aesthetics from the faux-Polynesian creations of white Mainland interlopers (a.k.a. "Haoles").

Origin Story

History credits the Texas-born, New Orleans-raised Ernest Raymond Beaumont Gantt with "inventing" tiki culture. If that name doesn't ring a bell, it's probably because he's better known by his chosen moniker—the one to which he had it legally changed—Donn Beach. Beach claims to have spent his early adulthood working aboard ships traveling through the South Seas, where he allegedly gained an affinity for the Polynesian aesthetic. He also wove tales of his years spent running rum to Prohibition-era America. You have to take a lot of that with a grain of salt, as the erstwhile Mr. Gantt was known to, um . . . exaggerate.

But what's an undisputable fact is that in 1934—mere months after booze became legal again stateside—he opened, in Hollywood, Don's Beachcomber, essentially the first known tiki bar. His clientele soon began referring to him as Don the Beachcomber, which ultimately prompted the legal name change (albeit with an extra "n").

The real heyday for the tiki genre began in the years immediately following World War II. Returning GIs who served in the Pacific Theater gained an affinity for the islands. Why they did is a bit of a mystery since they were immersed in a devastatingly bloody war there. Can you get Stockholm Syndrome from a place?

Ultimately, enthusiasm for the tiki scene waned by the seventies and all but vanished in the eighties. And, in the spirit of "everything that's old is new again," the subculture began enjoying a full-blown resurgence by the end of the first decade of the twenty-first century.

There remains very little about the scene that's "authentic," and that's just the way I like it. I want my tiki to be authentically inauthentic. Tiki bars are meant to provide absolute escapes from the outside world. So why on earth would anyone want to see the outside world through windows—especially if it's still light out? And why would anyone want to be reminded that it's light out by keeping the interior as brightly lit as a suburban bakery? Not to mention, why would anyone want to actually be able to "see" other people or be seen? There's no better way to feel anonymous and undisturbed than shrouded in shadows in an indoor phony Pacific Island paradise.

My inclination to escape, sometimes even from myself, is consistent with the "preference for solitude" that Dr. Cheek identified.

"Some people are quite distressed at being alone," Dr. Cheek says, noting that introverts thrive in these escapist situations, with our observational skills fully in tune. "Introverts are forced to behold the spectacle of the extroverts. And plus, introverts are thoughtful and often pause to check. Introverts know a lot more about extroverts, but extroverts don't know much about introverts."

Frankie's Tiki Room

One of my favorite rituals of late happens to be in one of my least favorite cities in the world, one where I'm forced to observe the extroverted underbelly virtually every hour of the day. I've been to Las Vegas more than any human should be allowed. Unfortunately, I work in a business in which everyone making decisions thinks Sin City is the best place to host conferences and trade shows. Therefore, since 2003, I've been to Vegas no fewer than sixty times. And that's no exaggeration. I don't know the exact number because I stopped counting after sixty.

As much as I loathe this city, I've made my peace with it. After nearly two decades of multiple visits per year, I've been able to figure out one thing I actually like about the place and I make sure I get the chance to do that while I'm there: have a few drinks at Frankie's Tiki Room.

Frankie's is an escape in every sense. Both Golden Tiki and Frankie's are located off the Strip, but Frankie's is much farther off the Strip. The guests who are there really *want* to be there. Also, it's much darker. It'd be pitch black if not for the candles on the cabaret-style and banquette two-tops and relatively small communal table—not to mention the glow of the video slot machine bars because Vegas, baby! The illumination is just enough to make the Polynesian-pop décor visible. And what a visual feast it is. Aside from the usual wood-carved tikis and dangling petrified puffer fish and bamboo up the wazoo, the ceiling is covered in a fishing net and assorted oddities. Among those is half of a broken surfboard, which appears to have met the business end of some shark's teeth. Next to that is the bloody torso of a mannequin, very likely the woman who was riding that surfboard when Bruce the Great White paid her a visit.

It's home to the greatest jukebox I've encountered, full of surf rock, a bit of tropical exotica, some rockabilly, and a touch of garage rock. I didn't have to spend a dollar on it because all of the selections that everyone else made were nothing short of perfect.

And if you're a smoker, this is your place because it's one of the few remaining tiki bars in the US where it's not banned. I do not smoke and, I'll admit, I'm not crazy about that aspect of Frankie's, but I find it to be a small price to pay. I've learned to travel with an extra change of clothes, since whatever I'm wearing when I go to Frankie's is going to end up smelling like a dirty ashtray before I finish a single drink.

I've also learned to mitigate that situation by heading to Frankie's in the early afternoon on a weekday when there are fewer people there. There's no shame in day drinking—especially not in Las Vegas of all places. And when you consider that Frankie's is open twenty-four hours a day—an extreme rarity or, perhaps, an absolute anomaly for a tiki bar—day drinking (even early-morning drinking for that matter) is downright encouraged.

If you're put off by the laissez-faire tobacco policy at this Vegas institution, don't worry. You still have just about every other tiki bar in the world.

That California Trip

California pretty much invented the concept of a smoking ban and, as it happens, the tiki bar itself. I'll make up any cover story to fly to Los Angeles regularly, but more often than not my real, secret reason for heading west is that I want to spend a few hours hiding in the dark at some of my favorite, old-school establishments.

North Hollywood's Tonga Hut is everything I want and more in a tiki bar. It's exactly where any sensible introvert should want to be at around 6:30 p.m. on a Tuesday night. It absolutely nails the darkness thing. It's easy to get lost there. A person you're trying to avoid could be sitting right next to you at the bar and they probably wouldn't be able to make out that it's you.

And I know this makes zero sense and is a total oxymoron, but on a recent visit when there were around twenty people scattered throughout the space—on stools or in the green vinyl-seated, bamboo-enhanced booths—the vibe was quietly noisy. There's really no other way to describe the mix of conversations and music. People seemed to be using their indoor voices throughout. I could discern what everyone was talking about, and I was interested. Folks often rate a place for its "great people-watching." Tonga Hut offers unparalleled "people-hearing." And that's even with the music playing, at a subdued, yet still pleasantly audible level—about a three.

About that music: I've already told you what I 100 percent *don't* want to hear in a tiki bar (or any other kind of bar, for that matter). What I do want to hear: punk, post-punk, new wave, and the genres to which all of those owe a certain debt: surf rock, garage, rockabilly, and soul.

Surf guitar is a new passion of mine, one I gained from my immersion into the tiki scene. I discovered what would become some of my favorite bands from live sets at Tiki Oasis, the annual San Diego event that's the largest mid-century–inspired, Polynesian-pop weekender in the world. This erstwhile eighties punk developed a greater appreciation for the style when I learned that it's essentially a form of proto-punk—just like garage and rockabilly. In the time it took me to finish Tonga Hut's Old Skool Zombie (a strong AF combination of four kinds of rum, apricot brandy, and a touch of passion fruit), I'd heard everything from Love & Rockets and the Cramps to OG rockabilly artist Wanda Jackson.

There's a similar playlist at El Segundo's Purple Orchid—a newer, tropically inspired joint that went full tiki in 2001—that offers more sprawl, a stage for live acts, and a pool table with all of the typical South Pacific trappings (including the ubiquitous petrified blowfish dangling from the ceiling). Purple Orchid's less cloistered and "nook-y" than Tonga Hut and the bar itself is considerably longer, but there are enough two-tops against the wall to not make me feel bad about sitting at a table rather than on a stool. A corner banquette is perfect for those times that you have to be around people.

My only real quibbles, aside from the incongruous pool table, are that it's more brightly lit than Tonga Hut—although still dark enough for me to feel at peace—and there's a completely unnecessary flat-screen TV on the wall at the back of the stage.

But the drinks and music make up for it. As I nursed the Curious George (an indeed curious banana-and-rum concoction), the speakers entertained me with "Teenage Lobotomy" by the Ramones, "Primary" by the Cure, and the soul classic "What a Wonderful World" by Sam Cooke.

Purple Orchid's proximity to LAX makes it an ideal first stop for those who've just arrived in town or, even better, the perfect place to get good and liquored up on overproof rum-based cocktails so you can pass out on your red-eye out of La La Land and avoid Bible-thumping seatmates trying to save your soul.

POLYNESIAN PILE DRIVER

Serves: 1

You can avoid going out completely if you mix these from the comfort of your own home. Just remember to stock up on those tiny bamboo umbrellas! These two cocktails come courtesy of Frankie's Tiki Room in Las Vegas.

Ice (enough to fill the glass)

1 ounce Pyrat XO rum

½ ounce Cruzan pineapple rum

½ ounce Cruzan 151-proof rum

1 ounce hibiscus syrup

½ ounce lime juice

Club soda (to top off)

Sugar cane stick (for garnish)

Fill a Double Old Fashioned glass with ice, then add rums, hibiscus syrup, and lime juice. Top off with club soda. Pour contents into a cocktail shaker and, without shaking, repour into the glass. Garnish with a sugar cane stick.

SURF DRAGON

Serves: 1

If you pay an extra twenty-five bucks, Frankie's lets you keep the awesome dragon mug in which it's meant to be served.

1½ ounces Cruzan gold rum

½ ounce 151-proof rum

¾ ounce violette liqueur

½ ounce Carpano Bianco dry vermouth

½ ounce orgeat syrup

½ ounce lemon juice

2 dashes Fee Brothers aromatic bitters

2 ounces strawberry nectar

Ice (enough to fill the shaker)

Pineapple and Luxardo cherry (for garnish)

Combine all of the ingredients in a cocktail shaker and shake. Serve in the official Surf Dragon mug or a glass and garnish with a pineapple and Luxardo cherry.

HALAKAHIKI MESQUITIKI

Serves: 1

Mixtresses Sonia Worcel and Catherine O'Brien are at it again with this very complex number. Set aside ample time to make this one.

2 ounces mesquite-infused Smith & Cross rum*

1 ounce Zirvenz Stone Pine liqueur

1 ounce lime juice

1 ounce pineapple juice

½ ounce Pierre ferrand Orange Curaçao

½ ounce falernum

4 dashes Elamakule Tiki® Bitters

Ice cubes (enough to fill the shaker)

Crushed ice (enough to fill the tiki mug)

½ lime shell, pineapple leaves, sugar cube soaked with lemon
   extract, and lime ash** (for garnish)

---

*   To make the mesquite-infused rum, put 2 ounces mesquite chunks in smoker and set at 225°F for 20–30 minutes to get some char on them. Put in jar with 10 ounces Smith & Cross rum until fully cooled. Put in bag and sous vide at 150°F for 3 hours. Remove wood and strain through coffee filter.

** To make the lime ash, place 1 lime, thinly sliced, on a piece of parchment paper. Bake in a 250°F oven until thoroughly dehydrated (it is okay if they are brown), approximately 45–60 minutes. Grind slices (including rind) in a spice grinder or clean coffee grinder. Sift through a strainer to remove the larger pieces.

Add all ingredients except crushed ice and garnishes to a cocktail shaker and shake until thoroughly chilled. Strain into a tiki mug and fill with crushed ice, leaving space for the lime shell. Garnish with pineapple leaves. For the fire component, hollow out your lime shell and add your sugar cube. Nestle lime shell into mug so that the top of the shell lines up with the rim of the mug. Ignite the sugar cube. Shake lime ash over flame to create sparks.

I'M NOT HERE FOR THE TOUR

(A QUIET CORNER IN A TASTING ROOM)

At the time of this writing there are nearly 2,500 craft distilleries across the United States. If you think that sounds like a lot, there are more than three times as many craft breweries (and the number that are both is somewhere around 500, perhaps edging ever closer to 1,000).

A large percentage of those have tasting rooms where visitors can sample their wares and enjoy drinking something that's truly locally made. How much you can enjoy it depends on the individual state laws, which, as you could guess, can range from generously permissive to downright Prohibition-esque—especially for the spirits producers (beer makers tend to get a little more leeway because their beverages are perceived as more moderate. This is a fallacy, of course, because when you're ordering a "drink"—even if it's a neat pour of a spirit—you're only going to get one to two ounces of it, compared with twelve to sixteen ounces of a beer. It's all relative).

Some distilleries are able to operate pretty much as a bar, while others can only serve three or four quarter-ounce samples to a single visitor at a time. When it comes to being able to take something home with you, some states let you leave with a case or two full of bottles, while many—until very recently—would let a person buy one bottle and not let that same person buy another one for at least a year.

If you're lucky enough to find yourself in a state where the powers-that-be recognize the value that distilleries bring to their local communities and economies, make a point to spend as much time in them as possible. Distilleries are a gift and should never be taken for granted.

Into the West

If you need further convincing, you might find comfort in knowing that most full-service tasting rooms are very introvert-friendly (after all, many of the people actually making the stuff you're drinking define themselves as introverts and are always happy to draw like-minded individuals).

I sought to prove that assertion in February 2021 by taking the most solitary trip I could imagine. I, like most people who grew up in the United States, bought into the mythologization of the Old West for, at least, part of my life. Yes, all that Marlboro Man, Clint Eastwood, lone wolf bullshit (or, more appropriately, horseshit). The movies made us think that the landscape of everything West of Omaha, Nebraska, was Monument Valley. And that there was a clapboard saloon on every street corner serving up drinks drawn from the rivers that flowed with whiskey. Okay, maybe it was just me who thought this.

In any event, there was always an allure to the West—particularly the Southwest—and I really wanted to drink like a cowboy.

So, I landed in Phoenix, picked up a rather long-in-the-tooth Nissan Versa in the Hertz lot—slim pickin's at rental agencies because most of them were dealing with COVID-era bankruptcy—and embarked on a 1,500-mile solo desert odyssey that took me from the Arizona capital city, north to Moab Utah, and south to Tucson, before concluding the journey where it began, at Phoenix Sky Harbor International Airport.

Yes, in that order and yes, I know, logic-defying, circuitous route wasn't the most efficient itinerary, especially since the aforementioned rental car seemed to no longer have functioning shock absorbers. But I still managed to live my dream of sipping whiskey (and other assorted adult beverages) alone in far-flung corners of the Old West.

But wait, you say. Weren't we still in the depths of a pandemic at that time? Indeed, we were, but apparently someone forgot to tell folks in southern Utah and the entire state of Arizona. My double-masked face attracted judgmental glances from the unmasked masses. Yes, it made me self-conscious—well, more self-conscious than I already was—but it also pleased me that it kept people from engaging. This was one moment in my life when I was totally cool being a pariah.

The first opportunity I got to take this (temporarily) reduced social status for a spin also happened to be the first distillery at which I got to drink indoors since that whole COVID thing began. I wasn't happy about this, however. When I researched Grand Canyon Brewing + Distillery—yes, it makes both beer and spirits—I learned that it offers ample seating on an outdoor porch. Unfortunately, I didn't do the same due diligence about the weather. It was 77°F when I left Phoenix and I stupidly figured, how much cooler could the temperature be in Williams, Arizona, barely two and a half hours north? The answer, had I bothered to check, was more than forty degrees cooler.

That deficit became apparent after only about an hour on the road when I witnessed the landscape morphing from the desert Southwest into something that more closely resembled the snow-capped Pacific Northwest. Damn it! I forgot about elevations!

Needless to say, outdoor imbibing was not an option (not even for the rugged locals, as nary a soul populated the al fresco tables.)

But I'm glad that the thin, February air of a town sitting at nearly seven thousand feet above sea level forced me through the wooden double doors with frontier-rifle-shaped handles.

On the other side of those doors was the tasting-room proper, bedecked with all of the beery and spirituous merch, as well as a small, standing-room-only tasting counter. Enter (and exit) through the gift shop!

The entrance to the saloon—I'm going to keep calling it that even though no one there does—lies on the side of the retail area furthest from the front doors. And this is really where the fun begins. Before you enter the dining and drinking area, you have to cross a rustic-looking footbridge spanning an artificial stream that sits at the base of a mini-waterfall descending through a wall full of river rocks. It's like the sort of thing you'd see in an old-school tiki bar/Polynesian-style restaurant before they faded from favor in the early eighties—only Western. And, yes, you are encouraged to toss in some coins, not to make your own wishes come true, but those of dogs (Grand Canyon Brewing + Distillery donates to area shelters).

The rough-and-tumble wilderness theme continues inside the main dining room, with high-boy tables made from sectioned cedar trunks and stools that resemble gargantuan Lincoln Logs. Horseshoes hung in the "good luck" position above the bar. A multitude of TV screens had a basketball game on, but it was unobtrusive enough for me to not have to label this place a "sports bar." (Praise be.)

I avoided the bar itself—God forbid I'd have to sit next to a dude who pulls me into a conversation about elk hunting, bass fishing, or why he thinks the novel coronavirus was a hoax—and instead opted for one of the high-boys. Each had three of those log cabin stools, which meant if I chose the one in the middle, no one would be tempted to claim any of the remaining seats (spoiler alert: my strategy worked).

Since there was a full bar and food menu—not all that common at a spirits production site, but it was a brewpub well before Grand Canyon started dabbling in distilling—I ordered some wings with three different spicy sauces (Indecision and introversion sometimes go hand in hand) and a creamy tomato basil soup served in a sourdough bread bowl. But we all know that I was really there for the booze, and I was excited to see that Grand Canyon still had enough of its Star Shine American Single Malt left to keep on its menu an Old Fashioned made with said whiskey.

Star Shine is fairly young—it spends about eighteen months in oak—so the Old Fashioned's hue was on the lighter side, let's call it pale amber. Its flavor, I would say, tilted a bit on the "nutty" side—in a very good way.

The reason that I remember this so clearly is because I managed to stay off of my phone and jot down copious notes. It's the sort of place that you want to let just wash over you, put your pen to paper, and see where that takes you. The few surreptitious photos you'd take would never do it justice.

Now, I'm going to take a slight detour into a little story, one that illustrates the adventure that is traveling alone.

Taking in all of the sprawling majesty of the Grand Canyon's South Rim the next morning put me in a natural beauty kind of a mood, so I quickly hit the road for my next destination: Moab, Utah, adjacent to not one, but two National Parks: Canyonlands and Arches. It was a mere three hundred miles away but getting there was easier said than done. After I drove about thirty miles down the only road out of Grand Canyon National Park that would take me in the direction I needed to go to get to Utah, I encountered a barrier blocking all traffic from proceeding. And my GPS wasn't suggesting alternate routes. Because there weren't any!

I noticed a flatbed tow truck navigating around the barrier and driving on the wrong side of the two-lane road and figured that if it was good enough for a much larger vehicle, it was good enough for me.

As I gained on the flatbed, the driver pulled over in what I thought was a kind gesture to allow me to pass since I could negotiate the incline much faster. I soon learned that he was hoping that I'd pull over so he could tell me something.

That "something" was the existence of—not two more miles down the road—another barrier. Except this time, it was a padlocked gate that spanned the entire width of the road. There was literally nowhere for me to go but back.

After I completed a U-turn, Mr. Flatbed came rumbling up the road. I was curious to see how he was going to deal with this latest obstacle, since an about-face by a vehicle of such size would require a maneuver not unlike Austin Powers's attempt to make his buggy perform a three-point turn in a narrow, subterranean corridor.

That didn't happen. Instead, the driver got out of the cab, walked over the gate, and *unlocked* it. I rolled down my window, expecting him to wave me through, but instead, he asked me where I was headed. "Utah," I answered.

"Oh," he replied. "You need to get to Route 89."

"I know," I said. "That's what I'm trying to do."

"But you can't get there from here. You're going to have to go back to the park and go around, in the other direction."

"How far do I have to go out of my way?"

"About 150 miles . . ."

"Ack!"

". . . unless you want to give me a big tip."

Yes, he actually said that.

"Well, it depends on what you consider big. I only have a twenty on me. I could Venmo you more."

"Nah, I don't do Venmo."

Wouldn't have worked anyway. As you'd guess, there was zero signal in such a remote, deserted place.

The driver—who I assume now works for the park—paused for a moment as I started to roll my window back up and resigned to adding another four hours to my trip.

"Twenty dollars is fine. But if you get pulled over, don't tell anyone how you got through."

So that's the story of how I bribed a federal employee with the last bit of cash I had in my pocket, so I didn't have to delay getting to my next drinking destination.

But if I'm being perfectly honest, I would not have minded the delay. The word "breathtaking" is far too over-used, for want of a better term, but I can't think of any other way to describe the scenery along the route from the Grand Canyon to Arches National Park. That drive needs to be on the bucket list of every introvert. Just you, alone in your vehicle for five or six  hours, with no one to fight with over which podcasts to play. And nothing but desert, giant red rocks, mountains, canyons, and more giant red rocks to keep you visually occupied for the duration. I probably could have made the trip in half the time if I wasn't stopping every fifteen minutes or so to snap an Instagram-worthy shot of some element of the stunning landscape. The only annoying part was that I never thought to make this trip sooner!

I did eventually make it to Moab, home to the brewery/distillery combination that bears its name. And I have to admit that I was pretty excited about this one because drinking alcohol in Utah is like a bucket-list-level experience. I just wish that I had visited pre-2017 to experience the Beehive State in all its restrictive glory (for the sheer oddity of it all).

In the summer of 2017, Utah got rid of its Zion Curtain law, which required many restaurants to put up a partition that served to block the view of alcoholic drinks being mixed and poured. Apparently, the sight of booze would melt people's faces, akin to the opening of the Ark of the Covenant.

And, for a brief period, between May 2017 and May 2018, all bars and restaurants serving alcohol were required to post an 8.5 x 11-inch sign in conspicuous locations that read either "This premise is licensed as a restaurant (not a bar)" or "This premise is licensed as a bar (not a restaurant)."

Utah has loosened many of its other liquor laws considerably in recent years. For instance, at the same time that the bar-not-bar sign law was enacted, the state started allowing venues to serve brunch cocktails an hour earlier than previously on weekends, state and federal holidays, and at private events. The time restriction shifted from 11:30 a.m. to 10:30 a.m. (And that's pretty progressive. There are still a number of states that will make you drink a virgin Mary before noon.)

But you have to take the good with the bad. Utah continues to find ways to deter folks from drinking. At the end of 2018, the legal limit dropped to .05 BAC, from .08 BAC—the limit for most of the rest of the country (and much of the world). And that itself was down from the previous threshold of .1, which dropped in most states in the mid-1990s.

It's certainly not without precedent. When I visited Scotland in January 2015, it was only a couple of weeks after the country enacted a .05 limit (England and Wales kept the .08 threshold). The tasting room attendant at the Glengoyne Distillery just outside of Glasgow informed me that he would not let me taste anything because of the then-new law. He explained the new definition of "intoxicated" thusly: "If you drink one pint of beer (at the typical Scottish level of around 4 to 5 percent ABV) and get in your car a half hour after you've finished, you're still legally drunk." Wow.

You'll also be surprised to know that .05 has become the norm throughout most of Western Europe—yes, even in those great beer meccas of Germany and Belgium. Some countries have an even lower BAC law. It's only .02 in Iceland, Norway, and Poland.

So maybe, as far as the United States is concerned, Utah is a bit of a trendsetter!

Luckily, in Moab, my hotel was only about a mile from the distillery, and I didn't have to drive.

Moab Brewery & Distillery lacked the interior Western charm that Grand Canyon had—I got more of a diner-y/sports bar vibe from it. But the toasty malt smell that permeated the air pleased me because it meant beer was being brewed (you'd be surprised by the number of places that call themselves brewpubs, but there's nary a kettle to be found).

Also, the place could have been a box with blank white walls and it wouldn't have mattered. The entire town is surrounded by towering red rocks and, as long as you were near a window, that's all the décor and atmosphere that you needed.

The availability of the distillery's Canyonlands Confluence Single Malt Whisky is extremely limited and didn't find its way into any of the cocktail recipes on the menu. So I opted, instead, for a gin and tonic made with the house Spot On Gin (that's what it's called, I'm not reviewing it!). It's a fairly no-bullshit, what-you-see-is-what-you-get G&T, not a lot of bells and whistles. Go to Spain if you want that.

It was the right kind of refreshing after about seven hours in the car. And it was the perfect accompaniment for my chosen activity at this particular destination: sifting through the hundred-plus photos of brick-hued mesas, ivory mountain tops, and the rest of the geological feast-for-the eyes that I spied between northern Arizona and southern Utah. Happy hour became "Instagram hour." I hope Moab Brewery & Distillery's data plan was unlimited because I may have cost the company its monthly allotment. (Sorry!)

I know it doesn't really seem logical to anyone who's ever looked at a map, but the next stop on my Southwestern odyssey was practically at the southernmost tip of Arizona, about thirty miles from the Mexican border in Elgin (did I mention it's a scenic drive? So, shut up and plan your own itinerary). It's about fifty miles south of Tucson and, oddly enough, Arizona wine country. Yes, it really exists.

Nestled amidst a string of vintners is Flying Leap Vineyards, which added "and Distillery" to its name in 2016 when it figured out what to do with its excess grapes. As you'd expect, it makes cognac-style brandy, but as you wouldn't expect, it's one of a relatively small number of American spirits producers that make grappa. And pretty great grappa, at that. Not bad for an operation that's six thousand miles from Italy and way off the beaten path in the middle of the desert. (And contrary to what most might think, there's a shit-ton of money to be made in grappa if you can find folks who want to

buy it. A fifty-three-gallon barrel holds enough of the stuff to gross Flying Leap about a half-million bucks when all is said and bottled.)

Flying Leap has more recently ventured beyond fruit distillates and branched out into whiskey—a smart move, as owner and distiller Mark Beres notes, because the ratio of those in the US familiar with whiskey to those who have any real clue what constitutes a brandy is dramatically lopsided in favor of the former. The distillery tries to bridge that gap a little bit with something it calls Frankenbourbon, a whiskey-brandy hybrid.

But Beres is also harnessing local terroir and making a whiskey out of Sonora White Wheat, a prized grain throughout Arizona and surrounding areas, known to make breads that help put most sandwiches to shame.

For a different taste of the desert, I headed up to Hamilton Distillers, makers of Whiskey Del Bac, in Tucson. Founded by the father-daughter team of Stephen and Amanda Paul, the distillery focuses exclusively on single malt, and its team smokes much of that malt with velvet mesquite, native to those arid Sonoran lands. Stephen previously ran, with his wife, Elaine, Arroyo Design, which made furniture out of mesquite wood. The distillery's tasting room and conference room feature such pieces.

Dorado is Del Bac's primary mesquite-smoked whiskey, aged in oak for under two years. I'm also a big fan of unaged clear spirits and it was a real treat to sip from another of its smokey offerings, Old Pueblo—essentially Dorado that forgoes an oaky respite. It was an even bigger treat to take a bottle of the stuff home and mix myself a bloody with it. A lot of brunch joints will serve you a Mary with a strip of bacon in it (among other massively unnecessary accoutrements like entire fried chickens, but that's a story for another day), but I think Dorado does the trick way better than a soggy piece of cured pig meat ever could.

And the smoke-averse needn't fret because Whiskey Del Bac also offers its Classic Single Malt, sans mesquite enhancement.

Del Bac also regularly offers its Distiller's Cut, a limited run—usually fewer than seven hundred bottles—cask-strength blend of select malts and different finishing methods. All booze

aside, the best part about visiting Whiskey Del Bac was the quality kitty time I was able to have with Two Row, the distillery cat. Distillery cats are a bona fide *thing*, so much so that #distillerycats on Instagram boasts somewhere around ten thousand posts.

I have two felines of my own at home and the very definition of a perfect day for me is just chilling on the couch with one or both of them—should either of them decide to give me the time of day.

Two Row took a deep interest in my tasting flight, and I was 100 percent on board with that.

Before I left the Tucson distillery—and the beloved Two Row—and headed back north to Phoenix, Stephen recommended that I drop by an up-and-coming spirits producer in Tempe, Adventurous Stills. He found at Adventurous, a bit of a kindred spirit. While many distilleries source their whiskey from another producer—very often the Indiana behemoth MGP—Del Bac and Adventurous Stills are very staunchly on the no-sourcing side. Everything they sell comes from grain that they fermented and then distilled in-house. (I personally have no beef with distilleries that source their spirits, as long as they're completely transparent about it and aren't trying to deceive their consumers about the practice.)

I'm glad I followed Stephen's advice because Adventurous Stills really is a hidden gem, tucked away in a very unassuming corporate park—far from the crowds that give Tempe-based Arizona State University its reputation as a party school. The owners really seemed to understand that sometimes people want to visit their establishment to decompress. The tasting room has a real café vibe, with a matching leather couch and love seat with a coffee table where one could just sip, read, and just be left alone for an hour or so.

The partners are a trio of mechanical and aerospace engineers—Chase Estrin, Kelly Lattig, and Jeff Reisinger—who built all of the equipment by hand. When they weren't busy engineering, they were keen to get away from it all and climb rocks, scuba, snowboard, and ski. Their dream was just to make whiskey that they could savor next to a campfire after a day's adventures in the wilderness. That part of it has a very Ron Swanson-esque appeal and, wouldn't you know it, everyone's favorite Pawnee Parks director's image graces the label of Adventurous Stills's Red, White & Blue Corn Whiskey.

At least 80 percent of the grain the distillery uses in its recipes grows in its home state and serves as the base of a diverse portfolio of spirits that also includes Lost Dutchman Rye, Peralta Bourbon—whose roasted malts give it some pronounced chocolate character—and Picket Post Vodka, which assertively challenges the notion that vodka isn't supposed to have any character.

But personally, my clear spirit of choice there was the 110-proof Peralta Moonshine, the unaged version of the bourbon of the same name.

At the beginning of that week, I embarked on a fifteen hundred mile road trip, thinking it was going to be my own time to decompress. But I underestimated how much I needed to decompress from that decompression, and Adventurous Stills offered the ideal venue in which to do just that. Even though it wasn't a stop on my original itinerary, I'm really grateful that it became an unexpected addition at the tail end of my own adventure.

Things to Do in Denver When You're Thirsty

I couldn't get enough of the West, so I headed back in that direction seven months later, mainly to see what was popping in Denver, Colorado. The trip first brought me to Laws Whiskey House.

I've often joked that drinking whiskey is like a religious experience, but Laws practically makes it the literal truth with a small annex of its tasting room that the distillery affectionately calls the "Whiskey Church." When it's empty—which it was when I was there—there's no better place to contemplate your many sins and thank whatever god you pray to for allowing such wonderful libations to exist and the opportunity to not be bothered by anyone while you enjoy them.

Laws makes only whiskey and is known for its single-grain expressions that showcase the character of each of those grains in their respective bottlings. There's a Straight Rye, a Straight Wheat, and a Straight (Barley) Malt, each of whose mash bills is 100% of its respective heirloom grain. The distillery's flagship Four Grain Bourbon comingles all of those grains with corn. One of the best sensory lessons I've ever had was sipping a flight of the single-grain whiskeys, side by side, to get a real true sense of how each of those ingredients perform and contrast with each other. There were several visual aids in the Church, including an array of bottles filled with each of the raw grains. A chalkboard offered a virtual distillery tour, detailing the Laws process.

Oh, and there are actual pews against the wall, so you'll never forget that this is a sacred place!

When I was done with my Saturday afternoon repenting in the peace and quiet of the Laws Whiskey Church, I was recharged enough to let in a little noise for my Saturday night. I headed over to the Family Jones Spirit House, which operates a full-service bar at the distillery. It hosts high, wooden ceilings, cinder block walls with 3D, Tetris-like cubes jutting out in various places, wood floors, and comfy tables spread out across the room. But the low-to-the-ground bar, reminiscent of a sushi counter, was the place to be. Gardening enthusiasts would love the place because it's well-appointed with ferns and other plants. I was able to partially hide behind one of those plants, so it was like I had my own mini-botanical sanctuary.

Before I went, my Colorado-based colleague, Stephanie, described it as "Jurassic Park." I will concede that it was quite the adventure, enjoying an Old Fashioned made with the distillery's Ella Jones Colorado Straight Bourbon, and then an honest-to-goodness gin and tonic, with its Juniper Jones Gin. And believe it or not, this perpetual party of one felt like one of the family when the bartenders started handing out shots of the distillery's Smoky Old Fashioned and iRock & Rye, served in cute, Glencairn-shaped shot glasses.

You may have noticed a common theme among these distilleries—aside from their relative remoteness and the fact that their locales are very much a part of their respective brand identities. Never once did I mention a tour.

I have nothing against taking a look around the production area, but after the first four or five distillery tours you've been on it becomes a bit repetitive.

However, if you have a chance for a private tour with the distiller or owner, jump at it. In group tours, the guides need to accommodate people of all knowledge levels, from the seasoned spirits aficionado to the newbie who doesn't know the difference between whiskey and beer. So, you're likely to hear the same "basics of distilling" spiel that you'd heard on the first two or three facilities you'd visited. One-on-one, it becomes more of a conversation and you're likely to get answers for only the questions you want answered. And, oh yeah, no crowds.

CHICKENSCRATCH WHITE MANHATTAN

Serves: 1

Flying Leap Winery & Distillery offers a clearer twist on a classic Manhattan, using its unaged Chickenscratch grain spirit.

- 2 ounces Flying Leap Chickenscratch unaged grain spirit (if unavailable, find a comparable unaged whiskey or "moonshine")
- Dash orange bitters
- ½ ounce dry vermouth
- Small barspoon Marasca cherry syrup (the liquid in which Luxardo cherries are packed)
- Ice (enough to fill the shaker)

In a cocktail shaker, add the Chickenscratch, bitters, vermouth, and Marasca cherry syrup and stir gently. Add ice to the shaker and shake vigorously for thirty seconds until the shaker frosts. Strain into a coupe or martini glass.

A RICE-BASED REFUGE

(SIPPING SILENTLY IN A SAKÉ-SOAKED HEAVEN)

We are entering a realm that is very near and dear to my heart. I'm a total saké nerd and even have gone so far as to get certified as an International Kikisaké-shi (saké sommelier) by the Saké School of America. I've toured numerous saké breweries throughout Japan (and a few right here in the United States as well) and I've written a book called *Saképedia*.

Peace & Quiet in Portland

Our saké exploration must begin in Portland, Oregon, which, by many accounts, boasts the largest per capita consumption of saké outside of Japan. One of the venues that has played no small part in that is Zilla, perhaps the best saké bar in North America—not to mention one of the finest sushi restaurants in the Pacific Northwest. Owner and head chef Kate Koo is not only an internationally renowned sushi chef with a career dating back to 2000, she's also a Certified Saké Professional through global nihonshu guru John Gauntner's acclaimed Saké Professional Course and she passed, with distinction, the Wine & Spirit Education Trust's (WSET) Saké Award Level

3. So, Kate knows her saké and takes it very seriously. And she also knows how to hire well because the bartenders who regularly do the pouring share the same knowledge and passion for this beverage.

The best part of the Zilla experience is that you don't have to be surrounded by groups of diners in the restaurant portion of the venue because the bar functions as its own intimate space walled off from the dining room. The lighting is calmingly dim, but bright enough to behold the sprawling array of selections before you. Usually (in non-pandemic times) there are no fewer than one hundred different saké offerings on hand—virtually all of which are available by the glass. And that's a big deal in the world of saké—one that's fairly unique to the Rose City.

It's not uncommon for most places that carry the Japanese (and Japanese-inspired) drink to have a handful of single-pour options and then a dozen or so more by the bottle only. Not only does that discourage trying something new (I mean, who wants to throw down seventy-two bucks on a leap of faith?), it's also not very welcoming to the lone imbiber. Even if you're feeling particularly spendy one evening, it's not advisable to consume 720 milliliters of a 15 percent-plus ABV drink by yourself in one sitting.

But Zilla, and a number of other venues in Portland, democratize nearly every bottle—thus, lowering the barrier of entry to the saké category for casual consumers, as well as the completely uninitiated—through by-the-glass availability. And, in many cases, if you're unsure whether you want to spend twelve or fourteen dollars on a four-ounce pour, there are intuitively designed flight options that present a smaller taste from three or four bottles, tied together by a common theme (and those themes and selections are frequently changing).

Grab a stool at the bar for a couple of hours on any given night (I'd recommend Tuesday or Wednesday evenings) and you'll likely be settling in for the best crash course in nihonshu that you'd get for your money. And even if you fancy yourself an expert in the category, I guarantee that there's always going to be something on the menu that you haven't had before.

If you're hungry, you can order off of the restaurant's menu—with happy hour specials on some nigiri, onigiri, and a few izakaya-style snacks. The bartender will be happy to suggest some saké pairings for whatever you're eating.

Be sure to have a notebook with you. Or at the very least, take photos of the menu listings of everything you're drinking. I'd more strongly recommend the former because you can record your own impressions of each selection and hone your palate. Also, when you look like you're feverishly scribbling in a journal, people are less likely to bother you (not that there's much of a chance of that happening at Zilla. It doesn't attract that sort). What's more you're likely to gain the respect and appreciation of the bartender when they see how seriously you're taking your saké sipping experience. They might even alert you to a bottle of something special that hasn't yet made it onto the official list.

The Warm California Sun

Nearly one thousand miles south of Portland, Los Angeles offers an embarrassment of riches when it comes to places to quietly sip saké. I'll talk about Lounge Ohjah in a later chapter, so I'll focus on just three places that have given me the most welcoming experiences. Sushi Katsu-ya, in Studio City, is, of course, primarily a sushi restaurant. But the saké selection is superb and there have been times I've gone and had only one or two pieces of nigiri just so I could sit at the end of the sushi bar and work my way through the compact, yet well-appointed nihonshu list. My favorite time to do this is during lunch because you can get nosy in the bright light of day. It's Studio City, so a lot of "industry" people eat there. Sometimes you might spot a few famous ones whom you'd never have the nerve to make eye contact with or try to engage. It just makes a good story.

Meanwhile, in Echo Park, there are two adjacent venues (owned by the same team, renowned saké sommelier Courtney Kaplan and chef Charles Namba) that offer markedly different, but equally enjoyable experiences. Tsubaki, which opened first, is more of a moderately upscale izakaya vibe, with bites like wagyu kushiyaki (rib-eye skewer), sashimi, and tororo soba (cold buckwheat noodles with salmon roe and yam). The saké selection is vast and if Courtney's around and has a minute, she's more than happy to offer a suggestion or two and help enhance your education, especially if you were able to snag a seat at the bar. However, there were only so many saké varieties Tsubaki could fit on the menu and so many thirstier Angelenos to satisfy, so the owners took over the space next door and opened Ototo, an expansive saké bar. It does offer bites—which the menu calls "drinking snacks," so you know what the priority is here. If you want a "restaurant" go to Tsubaki. If you want a "bar" go to Ototo. The list is always changing so you'll probably never have the same adventure twice. Ototo goes through so much of the stuff that there are several bottles with spigots dangling upside down against the brick wall behind the bar for fast, easy pouring.

The East Coast Strikes Back

Enough with the West Coast love, though. Portland may allegedly have the highest per capita saké consumption outside of Japan, but New York can more than hold its own on the nihonshu front. There really is little substitute for Manhattan's OG saké bar (if you consider the early nineties "OG"), Decibel, in all its grimy splendor. The place practically begs for lonesome libation seekers, as the underground space gets pretty tight, even with its predominant two-tops. The graffiti'd walls evoke the punk rock-ish Wild West-y-ness of the East Village's pre-gentrification heyday. It's one of my favorite places to completely disappear. Its subterranean location makes one oblivious to the time of day (though it's always going to be after 6 p.m. because the place doesn't open before that), and the space's noirish shadows will cloak you from the outside world and all of its insufferable inhabitants. You're going to want to bring a journal, a sketchbook, or a favorite paperback because your smartphone won't likely come to your rescue. You're essentially in a cave and, regardless of your carrier, your signal is going to be shitty-to-non-existent. But that's fine because you'll be plenty occupied working your way through the triple-digit saké list. Decibel also stocks a handful of shōchū offerings if you want to take a breather from the nihonshu and take things up a notch.

Barely a ten-minute walk from Decibel is another East Village izakaya institution—albeit a younger one, having opened in 2004—Saké Bar Satsko, an ideal counterpoint to Decibel for those who don't find the latter to be cozy enough. The space houses a trio of banquette-like tables, at which a total of, perhaps, a dozen people might be able to squeeze. If those are filled, the only other inside options are the six stools at the bar. There's one more table outside under the awning that might be able to fit four people if they all take a deep breath. There was a covered patio that extended out into the street that could fit another ten, but that was primarily a temporary, COVID-related solution. That's just a convoluted way of saying that Saké Bar Satsko is small.

Saké Bar Satsko

But that doesn't necessarily mean that it's crowded. In fact, as is my habit, I made a point to arrive at around 5 p.m. on a weeknight (it opens at 4) and I was positively beaming at the fact that I was the only person (besides staff) in the bar for at least the first forty-five minutes I was there.

Unlike at Decibel, the street is visible from inside Satsko, but unless you're staring out the window and gazing at the pedestrians strolling down East 7th Street—some people call that a hobby—you're going to forget that outside even exists. That's even more the case in fall and winter when it's pretty much already dark not long after the manager unlocks the front door. And graffiti is not the décor of choice here. Instead, you'll find the wall covered floor to ceiling with hundreds and hundreds of Polaroids of all sorts of folks who've Kanpai'd there—with some images that are not safe for work. It's a perfect alternative to people-watching, where the people don't watch back.

The soundtrack for the evening is likely to be a mix of the usual East Village hipster indie rock, as well as some hip-hop fusion thrown in for good measure. I was delighted to sip along to the beat with some Nezumi Otoko Junmai ginjo, packaged in its own 180 milliliter glass cup. Some salmon onigiri and pork gyozo complemented it quite well.

Hometown Brew

New York is one of the extremely fortunate cities in the United States to have its own saké brewery. Despite the growth of US-based craft saké making in recent years, great American producers are few and far between and for every new one that opens, another one fails.

Thankfully, Brooklyn Kura, in the borough of the same name, is not one of the latter. In fact, any entrepreneurs thinking of dipping their toe into the saké stream could learn a thing or two from Brooklyn Kura—for one thing, how to brew an exceptional beverage that rivals many of the Japanese offerings that inspired it. It's also a comfortable place to hang after a stressful work week or to silence the Sunday Scaries as you quietly ponder the five days ahead. It's only open from 4 p.m. to 7 p.m. on a Friday and 1 p.m. to 7 p.m. on Saturdays and Sundays, so it's not necessarily somewhere that you're going to make a night of things. But that just means you get to avoid the usual meat market crowds and the Bridge-and-Tunnels—who rarely make it to any of the outer boroughs anyway. And the Friday happy hour set's likely to be chugging three-dollar draughts at some sardine-packed commuter joint named "O-apostrophe-something." And the weekend day drinkers are more likely to be at a sports bar. Trust me, you'll be much happier sitting on a stool at the bar against the ledge on the opposite side of the tasting room or at the corner seat that's the farthest distance from another human body, slowly sipping a glass of Number 14 Junmai Ginjo or Blue Door Junmai.

If this is a vibe you enjoy (and you will), but wish you had a bit more time to enjoy it, make sure you find an excuse to be in Charlottesville, Virginia, the site of the East Coast's other world-class saké maker. North American Saké Brewery & Restaurant in the city's artsy IX Park (pronounced "icks" and not "nine," as I stupidly thought). It's open five days a week (you're shit out of luck if you're there on a Monday or Tuesday) until 9 p.m. Sundays, Wednesdays, and Thursdays and until 10 p.m. on Fridays and Saturdays. North American is intent on bringing curious American palates into the saké category by any means necessary and offers a wide range of fruit- and floral-infused varieties to help bridge that gap between the familiar and the unfamiliar. However, I'm a strong proponent of going traditional and North American has plenty to offer in that department, from its Real Magic Junmai to its Serenity Now! Junmai Daiginjo. When the weather's behaving, sit out on the patio. There's also food to pair with whatever you choose to drink, and shelves full of games that you can entertain yourself with for hours to tune out the drone of conversations that surround you. Tasting flights are available, so you can spend an afternoon logging several new discoveries and their corresponding annotations, while you challenge your intellect question cards from a Trivial Pursuit box.

SAKÉ 101

Now, I don't want to assume most readers have a Kikisaké-shi-level of familiarity with Japan's traditional fermented beverage, so here's an elevator pitch on the drink. First, it would be incorrect to call it a spirit because it's not distilled. In fact, you'd be much more correct to call it "beer" because it's brewed, much like beer, and it's grain based. That grain, of course, is rice.

There are different "grades" of saké, based on the level of polishing that the rice kernel undergoes. If at least 40 percent of the grain is polished away—usually done in a precision mill—the resulting saké will be designated a ginjo. When 50 percent or more is polished away, it's a daiginjo.

The polishing ratio—aka seimaibuai—is expressed in terms of how much of the kernel is left. So, a ginjo with say, 45 percent polished away, will have a 55 percent seimaibuai and a daginjo with 60 percent polished away, will have a semaibuai of 45 percent.

There's one more important facet to understand. Sometimes distilled alcohol is added in small amounts to the mash to achieve a particular flavor profile. However, when all of the alcohol in the bottle is from the fermentation of rice and doesn't have any additional alcohol added, it's considered a Junmai—or pure rice. So, a saké with a seimaibuai of 60 percent that contains that small bit of extra alcohol would just be a ginjo. If it doesn't, it's called Junmai ginjo, and so on and so forth.

Generally, "premium" grades—an admittedly subjective term—start with a 70 percent seimaibuai. The pure rice ones would be simply called Junmai. The ones with the added alcohol—remember, it's added to the mash, not the finished saké—are designated honjozo. The ones with higher seimaibuai, say 80 percent or 90 percent, typically would be called futsu-shu or common saké. And then there are varieties like "Tokubetsu Junmai" (Tokubetsu meaning "special"), that I won't go too far into because we'd be here all night.

One more thing. The saké varieties I've detailed above usually are clear. If you come across one that's milky-white, that's a nigori, or cloudy saké. It's much more coarsely filtered than the other varieties, leaving more rice particles in the finished product. That's what gives its fairly opaque appearance. Sometimes people will refer to it as "unfiltered," but that's a misnomer because filtration does, indeed, take place.

TO LIVE AND DIVE IN LA

If the last journey through saké culture seemed a bit upscale and esoteric, this next bit should be an effective palate cleanser. (Though some of the grungier saké joints certainly borrow from the more divey aspects of Japan's izakayas, they are not, by definition, dive bars.) The drinks are always going to be a bit pricey, and the food is always going to be bit too . . . well, good, for them to truly be characterized as dives. Now, I  know what you're thinking: "Great, another ironic fucking hipster who loves his dive bars." Trust me, the venues that I'm about to talk about are the genuine articles, not some "wink-wink" situation that replicates all of the visual trappings of a dive but boasts a dozen or so craft beers on tap and serves truffle fries. Those self-conscious places also tend to open at 4 or 5 p.m.—not uncommon for most bars in general—but if you can't day drink at them, they go against everything that I believe a dive bar should stand for (and no, I'm not talking about Sunday brunch places).

Los Angeles has had a long and storied history of being the unofficial day-drinking capital of the US (Bukowski, anyone?). And it makes sense because it's a city where fantasies are crushed, lives are ruined, and tables are waited on at night as aspiring performers and wannabe movie moguls chase their dreams in the light of day. When the day doesn't go as well as they would have liked, they end up on a stool with a glass (or three) in front of them. And time is irrelevant anyway because there usually aren't any windows to give you the slightest inkling whether it's the early afternoon or a few hours before dawn.

Introversion and a desire for anonymity go hand in hand, so it's no wonder that I'm drawn to the OG dives.

Most of the legit ones are concentrated in the Valley and its vicinity and some of them open as early as 6 a.m. Among those is Michael's Pub in North Hollywood, whose business hours encompass twenty hours of the day. I really wanted to check out the early-morning vibe mainly because I was really curious about what drinking was like before most people have breakfast (or even wake up, for that matter).

If buildings had a "central casting" this joint would be straight out of it, if you were looking to cast a "no-frills tavern." The floor is basically the bar's concrete foundation, maybe with a slight sheen on it. There's a pool table, darts, and a rather incongruous fish tank in a corner behind the bar. Dollar bills decorate the ceiling above the bar and there's an old, early twentieth century cash register in the back next to the dart board. I'm pretty sure it's just ornamental.

But I wasn't there for the visuals. I really wanted to hear the sort of conversations emanating from folks who drink as the sun rises—even though this was one of the windowless pubs that shields its patrons from the bright, shiny orb. Here's a sampling of the morning's discourse:

- "Uber did screw me out of 150 bucks because the guy said I threw up in his car. I think I would know if I threw up in someone's car!"
- "I hear we're going to have to start showing vaccine cards in October," said one regular, to which the bartender replied, "I don't think that's happening in here."
- "Thank God it's Friday."
- "I'm supposed to be working from home today." (You're in a bar. In the morning. I didn't realize the conventions of a workweek were even a factor.)

Eavesdropping was only part of the fun. I had a blast testing out some boilermaker combos I came up with on the fly. I noticed Michael's had a bottle of Skrewball Peanut Butter Whiskey (well, it's more of a whiskey-based flavored liqueur). I wanted to prove a theory that sipping it alongside a pint of Guinness would make it taste vaguely like a Reese's Peanut Butter Cup. It did!

A TV screen behind the bar played the local news and I was about to leave when a live segment covering a bunch of dogs surfing somewhere near Santa Monica came on. Guess I'm having another.

Another of the earlier risers is the cash-only establishment, Copper Bucket in Reseda, though its 8 a.m. opening time seemed damned near close to dinnertime by comparison. Did it need to open at eight? Probably not, given the fact that I was one of only three customers and the relatively sprawling space—the bar itself was long, with sixteen stools and there was ample room for electronic golf machines, one of those table-top, sawdust-enhanced shuffleboard games, and a full-on indoor firepit whose flue carries the smoke outside. But I got a sense that if management even suggested delaying the opening by an hour or two, the pair at the bar would handcuff themselves to their stools in protest.

The room becomes a kind of unintentional museum with its visual components, including a wooden mural that spans most of the length of the bar, signs with messages like "The customer is always right. The bartender decides who is still a customer," and a white statue of one Mr. Jack Daniel. I discovered quite quickly that Jack is the de facto patron saint of the Copper Bucket. As two more customers entered later in the morning, about twenty minutes apart, the bartender asked each of them, before they even reached their stools, "Jack and Coke?" If there's a house cocktail, this is it.

I saw the tap handle for Samuel Adams Boston Lager, which was exactly what I was in the mood for at that moment. When I asked for it, the bartender, in her smoke-damaged voice, replied, "mug or pitcher?" Did I mention that I was one person?

The movie buff in me was itching to get to the next place, Foxfire Room in Valley Village, which played a memorable role in Paul Thomas Anderson's 1999 multicharacter study, *Magnolia*. It's the spot where now-grown, former "Quiz Kid Donnie Smith" (William H. Macy) lamented the miserable life he'd led after peaking as a preteen. It's even located on the film's titular boulevard—though you'd barely know it because the unassuming, barely marked entrance is in the back, far from the busy thoroughfare. When I was at Foxfire

it was filled exclusively with middle-aged and older men—the only woman was the bartender. She greeted me with "good morning," even though it was about 3 p.m. Then again, it's easy to get confused because it's yet another of the dark, no-visible-evidence-of-the-outside-world variety. I soon realized that that was just her schtick because she said it to everyone as they entered.

The space has a sense of being frozen in time, that time being the sixties and early seventies. The brown vinyl banquette sold that illusion, as did the music emanating from the jukebox, which included a steady stream of vintage soul and funk, including "B-A-B-Y" by Carla Thomas, "Reflections" by the Supremes, and "Slippin' Into Darkness" by War.

"One-hit wonder," a very visibly and audibly drunk guy slurred (incorrectly, I might add), to no one in particular, adding, delightedly, "This is some real Motown shit!"

In any other bar, this individual would have been cut off and booted hours before. But here, he seemed like family. And speaking of family, the only person who seemed to regularly engage with him was a mobby-looking fellow who may very well have been making a good living as a stand-in for Paul Sorvino.

I ordered a Tullamore Dew ("Tully D!") Irish whiskey on the rocks, followed by a gin and tonic.

"You doing alright, Jeff?" the barkeep asked me. Oh my God, how did she know my name? It took me a few seconds for the logic to kick in: Oh right, my name's on the credit card I gave her to open a tab.

Eventually, the only thing that was able to pull me out of my daydreamy time warp was the appearance of a decidedly twenty-first century libation, that ubiquitous Skrewball.

This is definitely a situation that's highly enjoyable, if, as Dr. Cheek suggests, you put yourself in the role of spectator. It's among introverts' favorite pastimes. It's more than just "people-watching." You're still participating in humanity, observing and learning about all facets of the human condition.

If Foxfire Room lulled me into a relaxed state of retro reverie, The Scene in North Hollywood was the noisy wake-up call. Everything about it seemed bigger and louder. Like Michael's, its ceiling was full of dollar bills, but about ten times as many. The music—a smorgasbord that included Kendrick Lamar, Interpol, Beastie Boys, and even Elvis—was cranked up to the point that speaking was barely an option. If you wanted something, you had to gesture for it. I was sit-

The ceiling at The Scene

ting at the unattended bar for a good five minutes before the bartender emerged from the back room. He grabbed a bottle of Bud Light, pointed at it, and made eye contact with me, as if it was the only thing anyone drinks there. I raised the stakes and pointed to the tap handle for Michelob Amber Bock (it's still in the Anheuser-Busch family, so I wasn't being pretentious). I spied a bottle of Glenfiddich and decided, why not, I'm going to have the sort of boilermaker that few ever probably order at the Scene. Most single malt Scotch whiskey purists are probably cringing at the very thought of this combination. Sorry, not sorry.

If someone were to ask me to give the elevator pitch describing The Scene, I'd tell them to imagine if *Dawn of the Dead* or *From Dusk Till Dawn* took place at a bar in Dodger Stadium.

I also mused a bit about the irony of the name. The slogan should be "Go to the Scene to not be seen."

Equally dark, but considerably more stylized is Drawing Room, just outside the Valley in Los Feliz. It sports a bit of an East Asian aesthetic, with dragons painted in gold over a red wall—right next to those ever-present brown banquettes (the bars must all shop at the same commercial furniture store). And, in keeping with the running theme, you'd see none of this from outside because, look ma, no windows!

One Saturday morning there were about five people sitting at the bar, so I decided to sit on the completely deserted banquette. The music was low, so I was able to hear the conversations occurring in front of me. Well, they weren't really conversations, just dueling jokes (including from the bartender), most of which might be too offensive for me to include on these pages. But here's a sampling of some of the tamer ones:

- "When does a joke officially become a dad joke? When it becomes apparent."
- "A horse walks into the bar and the bartender asks, 'why the long face.' The horse says, 'Because the alcoholism is destroying my family.'"
- "You know what I like about Switzerland? The flag is a big plus."
- This one probably requires a trigger warning: "What's worse than ants in your pants? Uncles."

I chimed in from across the room with a joke of my own, which elicited some polite chuckles. Then I retreated back into my solitude, all of my social energy spent in that one moment. It was like I was cosplaying extroversion for a minute and the costume just didn't fit. The dynamic in the room, one introvert sitting at a

Drawing Room

corner banquette table versus a handful of apparent extroverts one-upping each other with their respective senses of humor, reminded me of something else that Dr. Cheek had told me. "There's a distinction between being alone and being lonely. It's one of the hard things to get solid extroverts to understand."

SILENCE IN
THE LIBRARY

Don't you sometimes wish you could drink in an environment as chill as the ones where you go to check out books and engage in scholarly study? Well, you can, sort of, in the genre of high-end watering holes that often dub themselves "libraries,"—sometimes in their very names. Such establishments tend to have literally thousands of bottles in their collections, many of which—

space permitting—are proudly arranged on shelves that surround their spacious drinking rooms (usually behind locked, transparent or mesh cabinet doors, so don't get any ideas!) And, like true libraries, your number-one objective here should be to learn. And you'd be amazed with how many hours fly by while you conduct your "research."

If I were to imagine a sort of East Coast/West Coast rivalry, I'd say that distinction belongs to New York's Brandy Library and Portland, Oregon's Multnomah Whiskey Library. (And I'd like to emphasize that said rivalry exists only in my head.)

Brandy Library is the more venerable of the two, having first opened its doors in Manhattan's TriBeCa neighborhood in 2004. As its name suggests, the focus is on fruit-based distillates—to an extent. It may boast one of the largest brandy selections I've ever seen in a single place, but its whiskey list is even more formidable. Its rum, tequila, and mezcal offerings are quite intimidating as well. So there really is something for everyone, especially if "everyone" doesn't like brandy.

Cozy, lounge-style seating with leather chairs and suede banquettes, carpeting in varying shades of brown and tan, dim lighting, and audible but not intrusively blaring music all make the word "parlor" come to mind. America definitely needs more parlors in which to drink. (We definitely don't need any more clubs!)

As one would expect at a place with "brandy" in its name, the tour through its menu begins in France. And, naturally, the French region at the top of the list is cognac. I counted nearly 150 different bottles of the aged, grape-based brandy named for that region. The next stop was Armagnac—cognac's cousin of sorts—with around one hundred selections from which to choose. Then we head due north to Normandy, home to Calvados, famous for the apple brandy of the same name. At any given time, Brandy Library's menu features between fifty and sixty calvados expressions. French brandies that don't fit any of those three styles are listed under "France-Other," while Spain, United States, and "Rest of the World" complete the menu.

If that sounds like a lot, we haven't even gotten to the twelve-page whisk(e)y section, spanning Scotland, Ireland, Canada, America, Japan, and "Rest of the World."

Trust me, you're going to be overwhelmed. I've been to the Brandy Library a number of times over the course of a decade, and I'm never not overwhelmed. But the good news is there's always a sommelier there to serve you and answer any of the four hundred questions you're likely to have.

And when that's not happening, you're left to sip in peace in your own cozy corner or while you wander around marveling at the shelves and shelves of super-premium spirits. There are even those moveable wooden ladders you'd find in some Ivy League library or antiquarian bookshop. But aside from that, "library" can almost be a misnomer. "Museum" would be a better description. Decorative copper condensers, the sort you'd find in the distilleries that make the stuff you're sipping, dangle above the bar.

It's best to go on a weeknight—weekend reservations are challenging to procure, anyway. You'll often read the term "people watch" in reviews of other types of bars, as if it's something appealing. Your eyes are going to have enough to do in the Brandy Library, between gazing at the shelves, studying the menu, and taking notes so you remember what you like and don't forget a thing about the experience. This is the place for "people listening," which is a far more fascinating pursuit than the optic one.

Since it's generally pretty quiet at the Brandy Library, with the gentle background jazz, the carpeting to absorb much of the noise, and the absence of jersey-wearing wannabe jocks emitting inebriated screams, curiously nosey folks (like myself) can listen to just about any conversation they choose within about a fifteen-foot radius. Though most of the guests typically speak in relatively hushed tones, there's always one person in the vicinity who seems to want everyone to hear whatever it is he has to say (and yes, it's almost always a "he.")

I was quite entertained by a blue sport-coated man of about sixty, trying to impress a woman of about forty (and, at his volume, likely everyone else in the bar) with his half-baked pontificating about world whiskeys. The bartender was politely humoring the bloviating blowhard.

Given the fairly stilted cadence of the conversation, it was an early date or, perhaps, a budding extramarital affair. This is just where my imagination takes me.

Where does yours?

During the moments that I was minding my own business, I was ordering calvados and Armagnac. Of the former, I started with Menorval Trés Vieux X.O. Calvados uses a classification system similar to other French brandies and the X.O. here means "extra old"— defined as six years or more in the barrel. Other designations include V.S. ("very special," aged at least two years), Vieux ("old," aged at least three years), and V.S.O.P. ("very superior old pale," aged at least five years). With all of the hints

of baking spice on the nose, a glass of this stuff is like warm apple pie—if you like your apple pie spiked with booze (and whoever wouldn't is dead to me!)

Once I was done savoring that divine selection, I decided to move backward in age and order a glass of Pére Magloire Fine V.S., from the two-hundred-year-old producer Calvados Pére Magloire. The brand's history dates back to 1821 when Dominique Magloire, an innkeeper in Normandy, gained a reputation for serving some pretty amazing spirits. Today, the distillery's owned by multi-brand group Spirit France, whose portfolio includes, in addition to several other calvados producers, a collection of Armagnac houses as well.

What really made this expression stand out for me was the striking hit of barnyard funk on the aroma. It just screamed "rustic terroir" to me.

Speaking of Armagnac, that's where I headed next (in spirit) with a pour of Jean Cavé V.S.O.P. It's got some pretty intense vanilla on the nose—which I absolutely love—followed by some intermittent notes of dark fruit—you know, prunes, figs, dates, and the like. Maison Jean Cavé claims roots going back to 1883 and the V.S.O.P. provides a relatively inexpensive opportunity to learn what Armagnac and that particular producer of it are all about. A glass of it costs $14 at the Brandy Library—remember these are New York prices—but you usually can buy a bottle of it at a liquor store for under $35.

Multnomah Whiskey Library (MWL) may lack the sort of low-key solitude the Brandy Library frequently provides, but it makes up for it in antique-y grandeur. There's an air of exclusivity to the place, which under normal circumstances, would make me hate such a venue. But this Portland establishment somehow manages to make the vibe an asset and a major selling point for those of us who fancy ourselves thoughtful imbibers (delusional or not). MWL's most polarizing facet is its membership structure. For $650 a year per individual, $850 per couple, or a hefty $2,500 for a corporation, you get to call yourself an MWL member. That grants you the privilege to make reservations for you and your guests (among many other benefits). Don't worry; the rest of us proles can still go, but we have to settle for walk-in drinking and dining.

And, anyway, membership is really only worth it if you live in the greater Portland area (or visit at least a half-dozen times a year) and can go enough to get your $650's worth (or $850's worth for you and your significant other). Plus, even if you decided today that it's for you, it's likely that you'll sit on a two-to-three-year waiting list before you can even earn the privilege of parting with a handful of C-notes.

Also, there is a loophole. Nonmembers can purchase what the venue calls a "hall pass" for $25 that enables you to make a reservation—provided that you're not planning to bring more than five other people with you. You get to feel like a member for two hours. Not a bad deal, especially for out-of-towners. MWL recommends that you book it two weeks in advance.

I got my hall pass for 4 p.m. on a Saturday, right when the Library opens, and there was already a substantial line of mostly people on standby, hoping to not have to wait hours to gain admittance.

As you've probably gathered by now, I've come to thoroughly enjoy my solo drinking (and eating) adventures. I've leaned into them and learned not to feel self-conscious about it, especially in places that many would call "a scene." But I have to admit, the feeling did briefly rear its ugly head while I was waiting for MWL to open. The line to get in was full of couples, double dates, and other small groups of people who seemed to enjoy each other's company. I could almost sense their judgmental eyes burning holes through me, the freak who looked like someone stood him up for a romantic encounter—likely because a better option came along—or, worse, the guy who doesn't have any friends.

Yes, this was all a fiction that my anxiety created for its own entertainment, but the paranoia dissipated the moment the bar staff unlocked the front door. (One thing I neglected to mention is MWL enhances its exclusive mystique by locking the door behind you once you enter).

In fact, the host made me feel like a visiting dignitary when he ushered me to an elegantly comfy armchair with its own mini table—right next to the active fireplace!

Similar to the Brandy Library experience, I was surrounded by shelves and shelves of bottles upon bottles—mostly filled with the "W" in MWL's initials—all accompanied by the requisite old-timey library ladders, against brick walls. The only difference here was that they were more than ornamental, as the ceilings were high enough to perform a trapeze act. (To be clear, that literally did not happen, nor would I endorse such a thing.) Chandeliers descended from the ceiling as a sort of final chef's kiss on a near-perfect space.

Service was first-class all the way. Within moments after I sat down, the bartender's assistant—almost like the opening act or the hype-man—let me know the specials, which included a fancy plate of charcuterie, with jamon (vegetarians and vegans, avert your eyes) made from pigs fed only acorns in their last years of life to impart a nutty flavor. Of course I ordered that, along with a twenty-two dollar (!) cheeseburger.

The super-attentive staff—including the star of the show, the bartender on duty—checked in with me frequently, chatted, and made me feel welcome and not the least bit lame for being by myself. In fact, I got the sense that they go out of their way to make every guest—regardless of group size—feel right at home.

Despite the high ceilings and wood floors, which usually create a massive echo chamber, the noise was pretty manageable. The music was kept low enough to not be a nuisance. I never could understand why bars that aren't meant for dancing crank up the bass-heavy tunes to the point that your endoskeleton is vibrating. In fact, the volume seems to be on a timer at some venues; as soon as the clock strikes 6 p.m., the noise amplifies. Don't they realize that just encourages people to talk louder and turn the whole place into some sort of auditory apocalypse? Is that something that Jon Taffer, the shouty ghoul from *Bar Rescue*, tells them they should do to enhance sales? Count me out. Thankfully, this is not the case at MWL. The Library very much understands and promotes the seemingly long-forgotten notion of the "relaxing drink."

MWL's staff strikes just the right balance between curators and creators—which every bar should strive for, in my not-so-humble opinion. That's why it makes sense to alternate between a neat pour (a nod to the team's expert curation) and a cocktail (an acknowledgment of their creative prowess). After my neat serving of calvados—I know, I know, this is a *whiskey* library, but I can't resist when I see the French apple brandy on menus—I opted for a smoky, whiskey-based cocktail. The cocktail selections change pretty much monthly, so there's always something new to try. The bartenders will be more than happy to mix you something bespoke if you just tell them your favorite spirits and your preferred flavor profiles.

The ninety minutes of my MWL happy hour of one just flew by and I really could have stayed there all night (if they weren't going to kick me out at the end of my two-hour reservation period).

There are few environments that are as conducive to just sitting with your thoughts, scribbling a few notes in a journal, and enhancing your libational education (a term I just made up), than at the aptly named Libraries.

CHOCOLATE KISS

Serves: 1

Portland, Oregon-based "mixtresses" Sonia Worcel and Catherine O'Brien are big fans of Multnomah Whiskey Library and were inspired by the Library's vibe to create this chocolatey concoction. It's cozy and warming, perfect for sipping by a fire.

1 ounce cocoa nib–infused Monkey Shoulder Blended Scotch Whisky*

1 ounce Knob Creek bourbon

¼ ounce cocoa nib syrup**

5 dashes Scrappy's chocolate bitters

Ice (enough to fill the mixing glass)

1 large clear ice cube (for serving glass)

Expressed orange peel (for garnish)

Combine all ingredients in a mixing glass filled with ice and stir until chilled. Strain into a Double Old Fashioned glass over a large clear ice cube and garnish with an expressed orange peel.

---

* For the cocoa nib–infused monkey shoulder, combine 2 cups Monkey Shoulder Blended Scotch Whisky with ½ cup cocoa nibs. *Very little* time is needed to infuse the flavor. Check after the first 12 hours (after that, it gets bitter). Strain through a coffee filter.

** For the cocoa nib simple syrup, melt 6 ounces demerara sugar in 4 ounces water. Add in ½ vanilla bean (halved lengthwise and scraped) and seeds. Place 2-3 tablespoons cocoa nibs in tea leaf infuser and steep in water or the syrup until desired cocoa flavor is reached, then strain through a fine mesh strainer.

SINGING SOLO IN A KARAOKE BAR

Warning. If you're an introvert—and I'm assuming many of you are since you've made it this far—you may actually hate this chapter. We're the sort who generally don't like to be the center of attention. In fact, we're not crazy about attention of any kind, because that implies that there are too many other people around directing it toward *something*.

And what is karaoke, but the average human being's momentary enactment of their deepest pop-star fantasy? When it's our turn on the microphone, we're forced to expel all of our inhibitions and vulnerabilities for an average of four to five minutes. That's the sort of thing that should make us run away screaming and hide in the bathroom for however long we're expected to be a part of the sing-along. So, it's inexplicable to me why I unabashedly and unironically love karaoke so fucking much! That's doubly true during solo visits to such tune-filled drinking establishments.

This is a relatively recent discovery. The realization struck me at, off all places, a speakeasy-style joint—complete with passworded entry—called R Bar in the Koreatown neighborhood of Los Angeles. The cocktail-centric venue hosted a weekly karaoke night, and I was lucky enough to be in town and staying at a hotel barely half a mile away on one of those nights. At the time I was just planning to go in for a drink—the bartender had mixed me a killer negroni on the previous evening and I was going back for more. But I thumbed through the song list, noticed that Joy Division's "Love Will Tear Us Apart" was among the selections and figured, "what the hell."

At the risk of sounding arrogant, I absolutely nailed it, with more passion and energy than I'd ever previously mustered at a karaoke gathering full of friends. I put my name on the list again so I could return to the stage in a half hour or so.

The place was packed, which I generally don't enjoy. However, in this case, the crowd was like a force field, rendering me invincible to second-guessing and embarrassment. I don't think I'm alone in recognizing that when we're at a karaoke party with people we know, we tend to hold back a little—assuming we're not entirely reluctant to perform (again, almost counterintuitively, I am not). We often hope our companions are far less reticent because we derive great entertainment from earnest, yet unpleasantly tone deaf, wannabe rockers fist-pumping their way through "Livin' on a Prayer"—lacking the self-awareness that they're making utter fools of themselves.

It's our own hyper-self-awareness (okay, call it self-consciousness) that attunes us to the fact that all of the laughing-on-the-inside that we're doing and silent joy we're mining from their personal humiliation could be directed right back at us come our turn at the mic. So, whether we realize it or not, we hold back a little when we're belting our catchy number. We might lean into our mistakes—such as our inability to hit certain notes—and spoof ourselves so the others know that our tongues are planted firmly in our cheeks and we're in on the joke. That's our armor.

We don't need to wear that protection when we're surrounded by total strangers. We could vomit all over ourselves mid-song and it really wouldn't matter. Sure, we'd be monumentally mortified (and more likely than not ejected from the premises), but we'd never have to see any of those unfamiliar faces again. And, once we overcame our temporary embarrassment, we'd have a great, self-deprecating tale to tell at parties (if we ever go to parties, that is).

The Alibi of the Part

That's a very extreme case and not likely to happen to any of us (but if it does, you should probably seek help. You may be a problem drinker. End of PSA). The point is, there's something liberating about not knowing a soul in the audience. That's when you bring your A game.

Dr. Cheek calls this phenomenon "the alibi of the part."

"You're putting yourself into a particular role and the people are not people you see again," he says. "It's like a performance."

Dr. Cheek recalls having a very shy student at Wellesley who was conducting an independent study to learn about her own shyness. The professor soon discovered that the student had, with two friends, donned wigs and danced on stage in a talent show at MIT.

"I said, 'how could you do that, you couldn't even speak in class?' [She] put on the wig and the outfit . . . she lost herself in the part."

Losing oneself in the part, of course, is easiest when you're traveling. The chances of running into someone you know drops from about a solid 50-50 in your hometown to about one in ten thousand in a strange city. That probably drops to about one in one hundred thousand if it's a foreign city.

The closer the venue is to where you're staying, the better. I've yet to find a more satisfying karaoke experience than the one at another Los Angeles bar, Lounge Ohjah, on the second floor of the Miyako Hotel in Little Tokyo. I've stayed at that hotel a handful of times just so I could finish my evening at Ohjah and hop an elevator back to my room. I've never seen more than ten people at a time in the lounge and the ones that are there are usually international hotel guests, whom you have virtually no likelihood of ever running into again for as long as you live.

There's also one of the best saké and shōchū selections I've ever encountered in a hotel bar (as well as some tasty Japanese bites, courtesy of the adjacent sushi restaurant Tamon), so really, where else would anyone want to go for a musical nightcap?

Every time I enter, I feel like I've gone through a time warp to the late seventies. It's a lounge in every sense of the word—comfy tan chairs, banquettes, and small, glossy, cocktail-friendly tables complement the six-stool bar bathed in blue and purple neon-like lighting. I usually stick to the bar because the lounge seating comes with a ten-dollar cover charge and I'm a cheap-ass.

The karaoke is pay-as-you-go. Flip through the catalog, choose a song (in English or Japanese), jot that choice down on a small slip of paper, and get a mere three dollars added to your bill. It very much captures the vibe of the karaoke bars in Japan, with very encouraging staff always ready to cheer you on. And you're very likely to witness performances that are far off the beaten path from the usual clichés. Let's put it this way: you've got a better chance of catching a business traveler from Kyoto bring the house down with an all-Japanese rendition of "Tonight Is What It Means to Be Young" from the 1984 film *Streets of Fire* (I speak from experience), than you are a frat boy powering his way through the aforementioned Bon Jovi mainstay or Neil Diamond's "Sweet Caroline," complete with the annoying "ba-bomp bom-baaaah" and shoot-me-now repetition of "so good, so good, so good!" added to underline just how those good times never seemed (in case Mr. Diamond wasn't clear enough).

Your anonymity is always guaranteed, thanks to Lounge Ohjah's strict no-photos/no-video policy—not to mention the ultimate kindness: a no-dancing rule!

And if you do embarrass yourself, the walk of shame is mercifully short. I'd recommend taking the stairs, to avoid the off-chance of riding the elevator with someone who just watched you emote over "99 Luftballons" after three glasses of saké.

HO CHI MALMÖ CITY

Serves: 1

You can tell by the name that this creation—another from the "mixtresses"—has a dual personality. The ginger and lemongrass straw bring it a touch of Vietnam, while the Brennivin or Aquavit offers a tase of Scandinavia. Since the booze base is Nordic, let's salute the greatest pop group in history—and darlings of many a karaoke catalog—Sweden's ABBA.

2 ounces Brennivin or Aquavit

1 ounce lime

³/₄ ounce ginger simple syrup*

1–2 dashes habanero shrub

Ice (enough to fill the shaker and glass)

Lemongrass straw (for garnish)

Place all ingredients in a cocktail shaker. Shake and strain into an ice-filled glass. Garnish with a lemongrass straw.

---

* For the ginger simple syrup, combine 1½ ounces finely chopped ginger, 4 ounces demerara sugar, and 4 ounces water in a saucepan. Bring to a boil and reduce to a simmer for 10 to 15 minutes.

PART III

IMBIBING INTERNATIONALLY

Up until now, I've kept things mostly Stateside because that is where I and likely most of you dear readers do the vast majority of your drinking. But I jump at every opportunity to leave the country and sip my way across many other parts of the world.

While I treasure the countless trips abroad that I've taken with my favorite travel companion—the woman who's just deranged enough to legally bind herself to me with both a marriage license and a mortgage—about two-thirds of the time I spend beyond the confines of these glorious United States I'm alone. And these are the times I truly lean into my introverted tendencies.

It's not uncommon for those of us of the inward persuasion to spend a great deal of time—free or procrastinatory—diving down rabbit holes. And many of those portals are history related.

It's no secret that being a history buff is a recurring attribute among non-extroverts.

It's especially true for the Thinking Introvert, says Dr. Jonathan Cheek.

"History is a great source of intellectual stimulation and contemplation for the thoughtful," he tells me, "and museums, like libraries, provide an intellectual oasis in our noisy social world."

I fully endorse that message.

If I had a patron saint, it would likely be Mark Corrigan, one half of the fictional duo headlining the British sitcom *Peep Show*, played brilliantly by David Mitchell. (If you haven't seen it, do yourself a favor and binge all nine seasons—they're UK seasons, so it's only a total of fifty-four half-hour episodes.)

Okay, please let me clarify that *parts of* Mark would be worth canonizing. Let's jettison the elements that make him a haplessly depraved, bootlicking buffoon who's unlucky in love and can never seem to get out of his own way, and focus on what he really is at his core: self-conscious, nerdy, and a wiz when it comes to history (sometimes his references are so esoteric, I have to press pause so I can look them up).

You've probably figured out that I like a good drink. But what I like even more is the opportunity to combine my cups with history, culture, and travel. And when museums are involved, even better. The world can never have too many booze museums, as far as I'm concerned. Or too many of the tragically dying breed of centuries-old, traditional pubs that are living museums unto themselves. We're going to start—where else—in Mark Corrigan's home country: England.

THE ENGLISH PUB

(ANTI-SOCIAL IN BRITAIN'S MOST SOCIAL OF INSTITUTIONS)

My first encounter with an authentic English pub was at a time when I was trying to convince myself and anyone with whom I came in contact—especially prospective romantic partners, who, sadly, tended to remain in the "prospective" column—that I could very well be an extrovert. I was twenty-two, about ten weeks from my college graduation (with a dim professional outlook, to boot). My friends and I had arrived at Heathrow that morning (an hour later than scheduled because the Irish Republican Army had been firing mortars at the runway in the middle of the night) and were hours away from being able to check in to our hotel rooms in London's Bayswater district. Fortunately, the nearest public house had just opened, so we crammed around a couple of small tables adjacent to a curved banquette and proceeded to drink. (It was five o'clock somewhere, that "somewhere" likely being Mongolia). My drink back then was all cider all the time, and I think I may have consumed half an orchard over the course of the week. The pubs closed at 11 p.m., which, back then, I found horrifying. In those days, my evening had barely begun by then.

My biggest regret about that time is that I didn't take the time to stop and actively appreciate my surroundings. When the pub banged up for the night—last orders were at 10:30—I was nowhere near ready to put my head on a pillow. A bunch of us would go to—Gasp!—a dance club, which was not bound by the same closing-time rules as pubs. We thought we were so cool, showing a bunch of multinational folks how to mosh—to techno of all things. Of course, we were too young and naïve to realize that we were in a complete tourist trap. It was Leicester Square for crying out loud!

Let's jump ahead decades when I now wish every drinking establishment at home and abroad would close well before 11 p.m. because I believe nothing good ever happens after 10 (and I need my eight hours of uninterrupted slumber)! I've returned to London some eighteen or nineteen times since that initial college getaway and I've learned to appreciate a far wider selection of classically British beverages—traditional ales, fine gins, and nuanced whiskies. And I've truly discovered the best ways to enjoy them—particularly in a quiet corner or snug in a pub that claims centuries of history, though it's likely been razed, gutted, and/or renovated innumerable times to retain its classic-ness and continue to tell a good story (even if some of the facts are varying degrees of questionable).

I prefer there to be some music playing—best when it's an eclectic mix of jazz, rock, and pop from all eras (punk and post punk are always great when served with a side of Beatles and Dido). But it needs to be at around a "three" on my imaginary ten-point volume scale (or eleven, because spinal tap), which is where those bass-thumping, sweat-flying, super-spreading, everyone's-zonked-on-Molly dance clubs rank.

Like all good historical institutions, pubs have been greatly consolidated or have disappeared altogether. The world needs to hold on to them for dear life, as they are international treasures and worthy of preservation. Luckily, gin has made a huge come back—as has brewing, though it largely emulates the styles revived by the American craft beer movement (even though many of those styles originated in the British Isles, long before scrappy, independent artisans on the other side of the pond coopted and reinvented them).

While there may be fewer traditional pubs (and exponentially fewer independently owned ones), pub *culture* is very much alive. For me, the great paradox will always be how I can enjoy solitude and peaceful contemplation in an institution that has, throughout its millennium-long existence, been the often raucous (sometimes there's sports, or at least people loudly arguing about sports) social center of whichever community it serves.

However, Dr. Cheek assures me that it's not much of a paradox at all, if I put myself in the role of spectator.

"You're not going there necessarily to be an active participant," he says, "it's more to just enjoy the spectacle of it. And there are some pretty lively pubs that are quite the spectacle. Being around people can be a positive thing, even for introverts, as long as they're not having any unexpected or unfamiliar demands put on them. If you're in the role of one of the quieter attendees or drinkers in a bar, I think that can be pretty mellow. And the people who want to be extroverted, you can see them, they're not keeping quiet—but you don't have to do it too."

Living Museums

England is home to more museums than you're ever going to be able to visit in twenty lifetimes. And it doesn't help that most of them close at 5 p.m. But those are just the buildings that have "museum" in their names. They don't include the stealthy ones, the establishments that don't market themselves as such but have every right to be mentioned in the same breath. There are few places you're likely to get as effective a crash course in the history of English drinking culture than in the pub. The walls, tables, ceilings, bars, and the edifices themselves usually feature enough vintage eye candy and historical artifacts—some original, others detailed, kitschy recreations— to satisfy the most rabid antiquities aficionados.

First, let's begin with the kitschy. If there were a prize given with that specific criterion in mind, the most likely recipient would be the Mayflower in London's Rotherhithe district, right on the southern bank of the Thames. And yes, it was named after *that* Mayflower. Captain Christopher Jones, who shuttled a gaggle of pleasure-hating Puritans across the Atlantic Ocean in 1620, has deep ties to Rotherhithe. It was the final resting place of both the storied sailing vessel and Jones, who died but a year and a half after he dumped all of the religious fanatics in Plymouth, Massachusetts.

The building occupies a plot of land that has had a pub sitting on it since around 1550. It began as The Shippe and was rebuilt in 1780 as the Spread Eagle and Crown. Nearly two centuries later, in 1957, it took its current moniker to underline its connection with the pilgrim vessel.

As you'd expect, the pub really leans into the nautical aesthetic. Model ships, paintings of seafaring scenes, life preservers repurposed as wall

hangings, and even a fish tank with live ocean creatures are among the stimuli that will assault your eye holes. Oddly enough, there are even a couple of petrified puffer fish dangling from the ceiling, something that would seem more at home in a tiki bar. (Then again, isn't a tiki bar just a nautical-themed watering hole updated for the mid-twentieth century and beyond?) You'll also encounter curiosities like a taxidermy stag's head, a random Ancient Roman-style statue, and an American flag extending over the river from the outdoor deck (in case you forgot where the namesake ship was headed).

Is it a bit much? Sure it is. But the crafts and tchotchkes almost form a comfortable cocoon to protect us introspective, solo sippers from any kind of unwanted social interactions. It's pretty much a place to hide.

A five-minute walk from the Mayflower (or perhaps you'd like to swim the Thames? No, don't do this) is where you'll find the Angel, a historic pub that's a bit more subtle about its history—with a focus on artifacts more than artifice. It's got the requisite photos and paintings of bygone epochs in the neighborhoods, but unless you asked someone, you might miss the fact that some honest-to-goodness art had been created right on that very site. Nineteenth-century American painter James Abbott Whistler—the dude with the mother—used to paint there, often on the back patio overlooking the Thames. Some of his art is on the walls there. When the weather's nice, you too can enjoy the view of what my friend Mike calls "London's greatest hits"—Tower Bridge and the Shard are particularly prominent from that vantage point. There's also a narrow, wraparound deck that offers some of those billion-pound visuals, but it can get to be a bit of a shit show. Too many bodies make it a tight squeeze, even if you manage to sit on one of the benches against the wall. I wouldn't call it a relaxing time for anyone who wants to get lost in their own thoughts.

I much prefer one of the many rooms on the pub's two stories, interconnecting like a network of catacombs. I found a particularly comfortable spot I'd like to claim as my own for all eternity: a corner banquette seat adjacent to a fireplace with rustic-looking copper buckets and some inexplicable tree stumps on the floor and a half-burned candle on the mantle. Directly across at twelve o'clock is a window with rough-textured, barely translucent Victorian panes and at about two o'clock is a snug, separate room that, once upon a time, was where women were sequestered when it was considered unladylike to be seen sipping among the males.

Even though my laptop and I are typically joined at the hip, this is the sort of place for which I'd always recommend leaving your portable computing apparatus at home. (I'm not talking about smart phones. I'm not a monster!) This is the place to grab a pint of Samuel Smith Taddy Porter, Nut Brown Ale, or Organic Lager (it's a Sam Smith property, so these are your best beer options), or perhaps a crisp London dry gin and tonic, open your Moleskine notebook, scribble with your monogrammed pen, and try to make some literary fucking history!

Pop Culture Pilgrimages

When I'm exhausted from a day of bar crawling in any corner of the world, I usually like to unwind with a little binge-watching and rabbit-hole-spelunking. More often than not, those two activities are intertwined. I can't get through ten minutes of a streaming series or movie without pressing pause to look up an actor, filming location, production crew member, or historical deep dive related to a show's temporal, geographic, or cultural setting. In London, this inevitably led me to Roupell Street, the setting of Daniel Craig-led James Bond film *No Time to Die*, the Tom Hardy–headlining biopic *Legend* (in which he played both Reggie and Ronnie Kray, the notorious London criminals of the fifties and sixties), and the Felicity Jones and Eddie Redmayne hot-air-balloon flick *The Aeronauts*, as well as episodes of *Call the Midwife*, *EastEnders*, and—my personal favorite—*Doctor Who* (the 1988 serial "Remembrance of the Daleks" to be precise).

Roupell Street has an eternal quality to it that makes it ideal as a backdrop for scenes spanning the pre-Victorian era until today. Cinematographers previously had to make sure their shots were pretty tight to avoid inadvertently capturing a stray TV aerial or satellite dish in the frame of a Dickensian-era picture. But now they can just CGI it out in post.

Roupell Street

The pubs in the immediate vicinity also look pretty timeless inside and out and they too have found themselves immortalized on celluloid (or, at least, as a bunch of ones and zeroes on a hard drive somewhere). The best example is the Kings Arms, which is about as generic a pub name as you can get—which very much works in this context because it's fairly archetypal and wouldn't have to have its sign changed to suit whatever time period it's mimicking. The interior is completely unspoiled (at least it looks that way). Even the wooden planks that compose the floor appear to have been trod on for 150 years. At the very least, they don't look faux-old. If you were to close your eyes and imagine "English pub," the Kings Arms is probably the visual your brain would create, having never even been there. The stools, the paned-and-stained glass partitions, the fire—it's all there. It's a truly inspiring place for creative pursuits—whether you're journaling, writing a script, or sketching on a pad. The ghosts that probably haunt the place are more than happy to be your muses. It's not like they have anything better to do. Eternity is boring.

Stick to the cask ales if you really want to maintain the illusion. I'm pretty sure the stout from Kent-based Pig and Porter or the bitter from Welsh brewery Brains is about a spot-on approximation of the earliest iterations of those venerable styles that you're going to get.

As devout a *Doctor Who* aficionado that I may be, I'm not always going to the UK to time travel. Sometimes I want to be in the here and now, and one of the most popular, awarded series of the 2020s, *Ted Lasso*, drew me to the southwest London borough of Richmond, home of the fictional AFC

The Prince's Head

Richmond football (okay, "soccer") team, which the titular American transplant coaches. It's a charming district, about as village-y a setting as you can hope within the metropolitan area of one of the world's biggest cities. The moment I stepped off the train I made a beeline for The Prince's Head, which stands in for Ted's local, The Crown & Anchor. Only the name is changed on the building. The white stucco façade, complete with the Fuller's signage—it is, after all, a Fuller's-owned pub—remains intact for the shoots. I like that The Prince's Head seems indifferent to that. Unless you were a fan of the show and could draw the exterior of the establishment from memory, you'd have no idea about its pop-cultural significance. It's not the sort of place that hangs production shots or tries to capitalize off of it by selling merch ("Mom and Dad went to the pub from *Ted Lasso* and all I got was this lousy T-shirt" sort of thing).

What it does have is quite possibly the best pint of Fuller's ESB that I've had outside the brewery in Chiswick. It also has what I like to call the "fuck off seat," a moderately sequestered nook whose very existence tells anyone who's not you (or your one or two companions) just that. It's a round high-boy table with three stools and a wooden beam that cordons you off from the rest of the pub like it's your own personal VIP area. The space has its own decorations, including an early twentieth century "Boating on the Thames, Richmond" picture and a fish-centric vintage advertisement for the town that reads, "Water is cool, water is lazy, water is lively. So the Riverside is the best place for July, August, and September." (I guess June could just piss off).

Despite the fact that The Prince's Head is a low-key TV star, offers a comfy space to shelter my delicate self from the world, and pours some absolutely spot-on pints, it's not even my favorite watering hole in Richmond. That distinction belongs to a place just around the corner, the Old Ship. As the name so blatantly tells you, this is another of those venues that fetishizes all things nautical. I think I'm becoming a model boat person because I'm discovering that I love to be surrounded by little wooden ships. Complementing

the visuals, at least on a subdued weeknight, is a music mix whose volume never seems to go above a two or three on my beloved, imaginary "ten-point loudness scale." And what a mix it was! In the confines of a half-hour, I heard Pink Floyd's "Money," "Turning Japanese" by the Vapors, "Centerfold" by the J. Geils Band, and the Troggs's immortal "Wild Thing." Under any other circumstances these would all be party songs. But at the non-oppressive level at which they were played, they felt like Sunday-afternoon-coffee-house tunes. Adding to the comfort was the seat cushion—on top of my treasured corner banquette seat—on which an early nineteenth century map of the world was printed (in case the ships weren't enough to drive home the global navigational theme).

A few feet from me sat a woman writing in a notebook, so I knew I was in the right place. (As the aforementioned Mark Corrigan would say, "She's one of me!")

But the pub still had more hidden treats to reveal. At the top of the stairs is more naval porn—another sailing vessel, this time rendered in stained glass—and a whole other, "I'm going to retire to my study"-type room with upholstered wing chairs. Wing chairs, I tell you!

And I hadn't even gotten to the drinks.

Since the place is so boat-y, I decided that I needed to have some gin. (They don't call the higher-proof versions "navy strength" for nothing.) But there's a wonderful selection of Young's ales, now part of the Marston's brewery and pub family of businesses.

I opted for a double gin and tonic—double on the gin, not so much on the tonic—made with Beckett's London Dry Gin from nearby Kingston upon Thames. In addition to England-grown juniper and some other conventional gin botanicals, Beckett's features some locally grown mint.

I was stoked that The Old Ship serves its G&Ts in the bulbous goblet glass popularized by bartenders in Spain. Twenty years ago, no one could have ever imagined that the two-ingredient, quinine-forward refresher could be elevated to such an elegant experience, but here we are!

There seems to be a tradition in British pubs to hand you the glass with the gin poured over the ice (with garnish, usually a lime or lemon wedge) and the single-serve bottle of Fever-Tree tonic to add yourself. It might sound like the bartender's just being lazy, but they're actually being very accommodating. They're allowing the guest to experiment and find what they think is the correct ratio. I'm still trying to figure that out because I've had a wide range of gin-to-tonic proportions and have loved them all. This never-ending trial-and-error is all part of the ritual and the ongoing journey. It's definitely an engaging project for the Thinking Introvert side of me.

Town and Country

As much as London and its many districts and boroughs are my happy place and international home away from home, it, like New York City and other major densely populated metropolises is, for all intents and purposes, its own country. Just as getting a complete picture of the Empire State requires you to venture well beyond the Big Apple's five boroughs and to areas that border Canada, Massachusetts, Vermont, Connecticut, New Jersey, Pennsylvania, and even Ohio, experiencing English pub life actually means getting into England's storied countryside.

A quintessential example, and one only about a ninety-minute train ride from London, is county Hampshire, whose southernmost section is on the northern coast of the English Channel. It's home to Southampton, known as a port for both commercial shipping vessels, as well as cruise liners. It's from there that the Titanic made its maiden—

well, only—voyage. My London-based friend, Mike Mansbridge, is originally from there and his parents, Sue and Dave Mansbridge, were generous enough to give me the lay of the land, especially as far as pub-going was concerned.

Hampshire's New Forest National Park—which straddles counties Hampshire and Wiltshire, is quite picturesque and everything you imagine when you think "English countryside"—rolling, verdant fields, thatched-roof structures, and farm animals (idyllic, as the kids would say, AF). But beyond the usual sheep, goats, and cows you're likely to encounter among the barnyards, you're also very likely to run into quite a few ponies and donkeys. And I'm not talking about the fenced-in field-plowing varieties. These beasts are just trotting about, untethered, across roads and through villages. They occupy a space somewhere between wild and domestic. Technically, they're owned by New Forest commoners—people who have "rights of pasture" over the lands within New Forest. That means the ponies have the right of way to graze wherever they roam, and the townsfolk don't have the right to shoo them away (some towns have garbage cans with small openings and "pony-proof trash bin" written on them). That means the ponies can start chewing on whatever's decomposing in the bin and upset their diets and the overall balance of nature. There are reportedly around 5,000 of them wandering about. I had close encounters with a few dozen of them in the space of an afternoon.

Sometimes they might even poke their heads through an open pub window.

My first stop, the Green Dragon, looked like it was straight out of Hobbiton (could the namesake dragon be Smaug?), mainly thanks to the previously

mentioned thatched roof. It's in a Hampshire town called Brook (because the ponies have to drink somewhere), exactly what's in your mind's eye when someone says "country." And it's the epitome of an English Sunday afternoon hang, with perfectly poured pints—I had a refreshingly balanced 6X Original Ale from the 150-year-old Wadworth Brewery in neighboring county Wiltshire—gently creaking floorboards, music turned down to a "three" (I'm realizing that this is the sweet spot), and no fucking TV screens! It's also home to one of the cutest snugs I've seen, offering a cozy hiding place (provided no one else is in there). I could stare out the windows and watch the ponies and donkeys graze all day.

Since we're on the topic of farm animals, there's really no better way to segue into the next destination on this rural escape: the Lamb. There are so many things to love about this pub, but the best has got to be the fact that it's in a town called, I kid you not, Nomansland! I just love that on so many levels. First off, sign me up for any place whose name is evocative of a world without people (even if that wasn't the intent). It also makes me think of the space between opposing trenches in Belgium during World War I. No such battles occurred here, but in my daydreams, I picture myself in a trench, fending off an army of encroaching extroverts threatening to contaminate my solitude.

The interior of the Lamb features some of my favorite décor—an array of wood-burning stoves (I just can't get enough of them), a chessboard on the wall, and a bunch of other mounted items that seem  to lack any rhyme or reason for being there: a coffee table book on classic cars, a portrait of a bulldog dressed like a Beefeater, and frames full of random, three-dimensional ceramic heads. Among them, I was able to recognize Laurel and Hardy, Charlie Chaplin, Sherlock Holmes, Henry VIII, a chef, and a pirate. The rest flew way over my head. Identifying them was a nice diversion as I downed a pint of Doom Bar Amber Ale from Sharp's Brewery in Cornwall (delicious, cookie-like malt) and whistled along to Peter, Bjorn & John's "Young Folks" (at the sweet-spot volume!)

If you can't get enough of the farm aesthetic, you'll be in for a real treat in a small Hampshire village called Fritham. The Royal Oak pub, which sits on actual farmland, is another of the thatched-roof variety, albeit a bit more pocket-sized than the previously mentioned venues. But the size isn't an issue in the spring, summer, and fall, as there is ample seating on the sprawling grounds. It's very dog friendly and the afternoon I was there I saw about a dozen canines playfully frolicking with one another. There was also a live band playing American-style country music, which was not exactly what I was expecting in *this* country.

To escape all of that, there's always the compact back room, which offers a decidedly calming vibe with a cross between a brick oven and wood-burning stove (complete with antique bellows) and what looks like a small church pew next to it. Near the bar, the walls showcase lithographs and watercolors of pastoral hunting scenes, involving everything from bucks to ducks.

Since it's a bit of a hole in the wall, you could very well become the mayor of the pub if you play your cards right. If I were mayor, I'd immediately pass a law that everyone has to leave me alone and let me sip my pint of Flack's

Double Drop—an absolutely cracking classic bitter from the Flack Manor Brewery in Romsey, Hampshire, that's got a deep amber color and so much bready malt character that it's the closest thing to comfort food that you'll get in an ale.

It's great fortification against the forces of darkness, especially if a visit to the town of Burley is on the agenda. It's a village with more witchcraft shops—crystal balls, magic wands, cauldrons, you name it—than you're likely to find in a city twenty times its size.

If you're trying to dodge a warlock's evil spell, the best place to disappear is inside the Burley Inn. The Inn is home to, perhaps, the best seat I've found in a pub. It's half of a two top in the side parlor that sits atop a tartan-patterned rug. I say "half" because one of the seats retreats inside what looks like it could have once been a space for a closet or a phone booth. And it's right next to a fireplace. It's the ultimate "fuck off seat" and one that would make the experience sipping an Otter Amber (from Devon-based Otter Brewery) that much more satisfying. I wanted to befriend some friendly witches so they could enhance the moment with a "leave me alone" spell, so I could become truly invisible in there. Unfortunately, I wasn't invisible to the one hundred or so deer I saw grazing nearby because the minute I got within twenty feet of them to snap some pics, they all decided to embark on a mass migration.

The Burley Inn

GIN AND TECTONIC

Serves: 1

Our friends across the pond are absolutely gin mad, so let's start with a creative twist on the gin and tonic—well, less a twist and more of an absolute elevation. It's a nice little ritual for the once-tired G&T. It comes from Shivering Mountain Distillery in the heart of England's Peak District National Park.

1 large ice cube

1 wedge of your favorite fruit (lime's always good, but don't be afraid to think outside the box—just make sure it expresses itself like a typical citrus fruit)

1 measure (let's call it 2 ounces) Shivering Mountain Premium Dry Gin

1¼ measures (2½ onuces) high-end tonic*

Fruit rind (for garnish)

Chill a glass and insert a large cube of ice (this will keep the drink chilled significantly longer). Wipe the rim of the glass with the fruit wedge (again, a rind-y citrus fruit is always best). Pour the gin over the ice and top with the tonic. Take some of the fruit's rind and twist several times over the top of the glass.

---

* As always, Fever-Tree's a popular go-to. If you want to go super-indie, grab Bermondsey Mixer Co.'s Tonic. The Mixer Co. was born at one of London's best gin bars, Bermondsey 214.

PINK SHUDDER

Serves: 1

Pink gins have become a thing (as have blue ones) and our friends at Shivering Mountain also produce an option with that rosy hue.

Crushed ice (enough to fill the shaker)

2 ounces Shivering Mountain Premium Pink Gin

2 dashes Angostura bitters

1 ounce Blanco Vermouth

1 teaspoon honey

1 slice grapefruit and 1 sprig mint (for garnish)

Pour all ingredients into a cocktail shaker, shake well, and strain into an ice-cold coupe glass. Garnish with grapefruit and mint.

DUTCH TREAT

(KOOPSTOTJE AND
SELF-CONSCIOUSNESS)

Remember all of that glorious gin we just talked about? Well, none of that would even exist without the Dutch. Because before there was gin, there was jenever, the venerable grain-based, juniper-enhanced spirit from the Low Countries that ultimately inspired Britain's most famous contribution to the global spirits market.

One of my favorite developments within the drinks world of the twenty-first century has been the renaissance, of sorts, of jenever, with a growing number of small Dutch and Belgian distilleries reintroducing their traditional spirit to the masses.

There are even dozens of craft distillers in the US that have released their own interpretations of jenever, though they've had to dub it things like "jenever-style gin" or "Dutch-style gin" to avoid using its official moniker. That's mainly out of deference to European Union rules, which recognize jenever (or genever—there's never been a consensus on the spelling, but I'll pick "j" because of my name) as a regionally protected product, produced only in the Netherlands, Belgium, and very small, specific parts of France and Germany. An American distiller could make something that's indistinguishable from a true Dutch jenever, but it still wouldn't be able to call it that. It could get pretty close, though. One of the most impressive iterations from this side of the pond is Geneva from Portland, Oregon's Freeland Spirits. But it still says "Gin" underneath it on the label because that's where anything of the sort gets categorized per the US Alcohol and Tobacco Tax and Trade

Bureau (TTB). It also helps from a marketing standpoint, because a miniscule fraction of American drinkers has any idea what the hell jenever is.

Which, naturally, raises the question: what the hell is it?

I'll tell you what the hell it's not: gin. I'm sure a lot of people will come at me for that, but, as far as I'm concerned, the only thing they really have in common is the presence of juniper. Even when there's a gin that's not a London dry style and dials back the juniper considerably, you still can taste the juniper and deduce that it's gin. Many times with jenever, you have to take someone's word for it that there's juniper in it because it's barely discernible. The ingredient is required if a European distiller wants to call it jenever. But the rules don't say how much of it needs to be there. (The same is technically true for gin, but there always tends to be way more of it than there is in jenever.)

The other component that distinguishes jenever from its English counterpart is its base spirit. Gin's typically is neutral, letting the botanicals do all the talking. Jenever's base contains varying levels of "maltwine," which isn't wine at all, but a grain distillate that is decidedly not neutral in character. In fact, depending how much of a maltwine concentration a particular jenever has, it can taste a lot like an unaged whiskey—with some spicy botanical enhancement. So, in many cases, asking what the difference is between jenever and gin is like asking the same thing about whiskey and vodka.

The pronounced graininess of jenever makes it the perfect companion for beer—which is likely what drinkers in the Netherlands were thinking when they came up with the notion of a kopstootje, their equivalent of a boilermaker. But it's more than a beer-spirit pairing. It's a complete ritual.

The bartender pours the spirit into a small, roughly two-ounce tulip-shaped glass, filling it to the absolute brim, to the point where it's practically overflowing. To prevent that from happening, the drinker has to bow down to the vessel—often with both hands behind their back—and slurp a few milliliters of the beverage.

Those who speak Dutch (and I don't) will know that "kopstootje" translates to "headbutt." And that's pretty much the motion that bar guests are making while ingesting that first bit. They'll then alternate between sipping the jenever and a glass of beer waiting right next to the tulip vessel (by the way, is there anything more Dutch than that flower?). I wouldn't exactly call the kopstootje a hip and modern trend. Much like jenever itself, it was much more common among earlier generations. However, it's starting to make a comeback, alongside the spirit.

There's no better ice breaker for those of us who suck at breaking the ice.

Keep in mind, though, that in modern Dutch and Belgian drinking circles, there appear to be two valid schools of thought on serving the kopstootje. Some insist on kicking it old school and filling the small tulip glass to the top and doing the full, hands-behind-your-back, nod-and-slurp procedure. I myself usually will err on the side of tradition when it comes to international boozy rituals, and I do think the bow-into-the-glass approach has a game-

like element that's quite appealing. However, the more modern bars will often pour the same amount of the spirit into a larger, approximately five-ounce long-stemmed snifter glass. There's a very good case to be made for this practice: There's some very high-end stuff being poured into those glasses, and you want to be able to actually taste it.

Here's the thing. Somewhere in the neighborhood of 70 percent of what you taste is thanks to your nose. That's why you don't want to waste money on a really good meal when you have a cold because the congestion will make everything taste like cardboard.

If you don't believe me, hold your nose next time you take a bite of something. Then release and taste again. See? Huge difference!

The thing about the snifter glass is that there's ample room between the surface of the liquid and where your nose meets the top of the vessel that much more of the aroma reaches your olfactory nerve. And the snifter's curvature helps concentrate and direct the scent right into your nostrils. So, when you're sipping the jenever/beer combo, the flavor just erupts.

One of the establishments that prefers to give its neat pours the snifter treatment is the modern cocktail bar Rosalia's Menagerie in Amsterdam—the brainchild of a pair of local hospitality-industry veterans, Wisconsin-born expat Rachel Bonnewell and her partner in business and in life Pepijn van

An upscale kopstootje

Beusekom. It also happens to be one of the most welcoming and friendliest places for traveling introverts. Since Rosalia's opened in 2017—I first popped in when it was but a week old—I've spent far more time within its walls by myself (well, except for the strangers around me with whom I rarely speak) than I have with my wife or a colleague. And that's the way I like it because when conversation's involved, I worry that I might miss part of the multisensory celebration that is Rosalia's. And believe me, the place hits all five of those senses.

Not only does the bar feature some creatively progressive craft mixology, but it also boasts a strong reverence for Dutch tradition. Remember, the craft cocktail scene is mostly a creation of the UK and US and the rest of the world generally follow suit. But Rosalia's leans into its Dutch-ness, thoroughly embracing the customs that defined local hospitality generations before bartenders started mixing ingredients in a stainless-steel shaker and pouring them over ice.

It's got an impressively extensive list of jenevers for use as cocktail ingredients, neat pours, flights of neat pours and, of course, koopstotje pairings. There's no need to be intimidated because the menu features numerous predetermined koopstotje duos, which, like the cocktails, change seasonally. A number of those might feature the beers of a Dutch craft brewery—I'm not talking Heineken here—such as Amsterdam's Lowlander. Lowlander Tropical Ale, inspired by the Dutch Antilles and brewed with dragon fruit and Curaçao orange—the famously bitter fruit from the Lesser Antilles island country of the same name—gets matched with an Islay whiskey-cask-finished jenever from Wenneker Distilleries in Roosendaal, Netherlands. It balances the brew's fruitiness with a touch of peat smoke from said cask.

I was trying to come up with a witty description of flavor and aroma experience of this particular pairing—mainly because the bartender was waiting for my reaction—and the best I could come up with is, "It's like sipping a fruit punch in front of a campfire." That still doesn't do it justice, but I only have so many words in my vocabulary, goddamnit!

And because creamsicles/dreamsicles make me weak in the knees, I had to try the combo of Lowland White Ale and The Stillery's Ouwe—a malty jenever distilled with a few off-the-beaten-path botanicals like hops and poppy seeds. The White Ale sports some of that same Curaçao orange that the Tropical Ale has, which brings the citrus component of the blessed frozen dessert. The "cream" portion largely comes from the mouthfeel of The Stillery's Ouwe. Does it really nail the dreamsicle? Maybe if you close your eyes. But if that's really what you're looking for, I recommend getting a Kohr's soft-serve vanilla and orange twist at any beachside boardwalk in New Jersey. Drink booze when you want booze.

And, since IPAs continue to be all the rage—for better or worse—there are plenty of jenevers that partner well with Lowlander IPA (and any IPA for that matter) to please the most devoted of hopheads. A few of the pairings that have popped up on the rotating Rosalia's menu include Lowlander IPA with one of the following: Zuidam Rogge Jenever 1 Jaar (one-year-aged) from Zuidam Distillers in the town of Baarle-Nassau, Loyaal from Amsterdam's Van Wees Distillery, or 5 Jaar (five-year-aged) from another Amsterdam institution, Wynand Fockink.

For a really nice counterpoint to the nearly overflowing tiny tulip/partially filled snifter debate, one only has to walk about five or six minutes to get to Dutch Courage, a new-style bar with an old-style mission. It's home to some 150 different jenevers and really goes next-level with its kopstootje combinations. All you need to do is ask the bartender for a recommendation and you'll be off and running.

Dutch Courage is one of two Amsterdam bars that are the creations of renowned Dutch mixologist and formidable expert on all things jenever Tess Posthumus. The other is Flying Dutchmen, which preceded Dutch Courage by a few years. Flying Dutchmen

© Ming Chao

Tess Posthumus

somehow manages the unmanageable task of being both intimate and majestic simultaneously. Whether you're drinking in one of the cozy lounge seats or on a stool at the bar, you will feel comfortably cocooned in a safe and hospitable space where the outside world ceases to matter for ninety or so minutes.

But there's also a sense that you're part of an experience that is much larger than yourself because the real estate Flying Dutchmen wears four centuries of history on its sleeve.

The building in which the bar resides began as a merchant house in the old seventeenth-century spice trade. The ceiling, which seems miles from where you're seated, features Renaissance-era paintings depicting the four seasons. The original artist is unknown, sadly. But it's been restored so many times, I'm sure many would take the credit for their roles in keeping the image intact. It's because of that ceiling that the Dutch government protects the space as a historic landmark.

Prior to its current function as a cocktail bar, the building has lived many lives. It's been a theater, as well as a meeting HQ for activist groups. It's played a vital role for the LGBTQ+ communities, as it's one of the first places where the communities organized and fought for equality in the country.

Community remains the operative word through its present iteration, as Flying Dutchmen can really kick the Olive Garden's ass on the whole "when you're here, you're family" thing. With the bland Italian American chain, it's little more than a hollow, bullshit tagline. But at the sharply appointed Amsterdam mixology parlor, even a loner like me feels like they're part of something grander and more amazing the moment they stroll through the door.

I made a reservation like a regular guest through the online booking system. When I arrived, Posthumus, the consummate host, greeted me by name—she had no idea that I was a writer or that I had any connection to the industry whatsoever. She makes it her business to know who will be enjoying an evening in her palace of potables and make them feel like VIPs.

Sure, most of us of the introverted persuasion don't like a lot of attention or for anyone to make a fuss over us, but I will admit that the gesture brings a welcome layer of comfort to those of us who are already way out of our comfort zones. I was a stranger in a strange land, but I immediately felt less . . . well, strange.

Flying Dutchmen   © Ming Chao

As Posthumus ushered me in, she said I was welcome to sit anywhere that there was space—it was 5 p.m., the minute that Flying Dutchmen opened, so there were plenty of open seats (but not for long)—but she strongly encouraged that I have a seat at the bar. But this wasn't a case of, "oh, look at you, lonely boy. Since you're only one—which, did I mention, is the loneliest number—we don't want to waste the space where a romantic couple might want to sit. Come sit with the rest of the forgotten dregs of society." No, this was a cordial invitation to a night of immersive theater. Yes, I know, it's a cliché, but there really is no other way to describe shelves upon shelves of premium distillates towering almost all the way to the aforementioned seventeenth-century artwork. (This is my Sistine Chapel. Booze is my religion!) The attentive bartending team will find out what makes you tick and then mix you up something special based on that (that is, if there was something that wasn't already on the menu).

But before they do that, they're pouring you a fresh glass of water just as you sit down. Now, why should you care about something as pedestrian as that? I'll tell you why I care: because it's the first place I've even been that serves your water with a tiny drop of bitters in it. "As you can see," Posthumus points out, "it turns the water a little pink." Not only that, she explains, it cleanses the palate and gets it ready for the many delights it is about to experience. (She employs the practice at Dutch Courage, as well.)

These are the sorts of moments you remember. Just let all of the visuals, performances, and rituals carry you through your visit and get out of your own head for a bit. That's the best piece of advice that I can offer you at the Flying Dutchmen—as well as at cocktail venues of its ilk throughout the world.

A new staffer came on board the night I visited the Flying Dutchmen and Tess graciously included me in the rookie's ceremonial welcome toast—with a shot of, what else, jenever!

I was worried that I was being gauche when I clinked with the barkeeper nearest me and noticed that the others' vessels stopped short of touching.

"Do you not clink here, I can't remember?" (I remembered the no-clinking rule being a thing in Hungary, something to do with the execution of thirteen Hungarian martyrs in the mid-nineteenth century.)

Posthumus explained that it was mostly pragmatic. "We don't clink shots because we might spill a little of it. When writing about jenever, always keep in mind that [the Dutch] are cheap and don't want to lose any of our drink."

Throughout my lifetime, I'd like to think that I've moved away from ethnic stereotypes. I grew up in a time that I wouldn't characterize as "woke" and, thankfully, most of us have evolved past that. In recent years, I've been hesitant to use a term like "Dutch treat," because, like everything that shouts out a particular nationality, it's rooted in some very negative cultural misconceptions. However, at the risk of overgeneralizing, most of the Dutch folks I've encountered have an extremely self-deprecating sense of humor about their bespoke stereotype, almost to the point that they lean into it.

Ask any jenever-loving Dutch national about the origin of the kopstootje ritual and you'll get the same response: "We're a notoriously cheap people and if we actually lifted the glass a little of the spirit would spill out—spirit that we paid for and are never getting back!"

Then again, that would never happen in a five-ounce snifter only partially filled. So, I have to admit, I'm kind of torn between the two methods.

One thing is for sure though: jenever is versatile as hell. It works perfectly in a cocktail, it's spectacular on its own, and it rises to a nearly religious level when it's served alongside most styles of beer.

Just like international mixology competitions have become a thing, I really feel like there needs to be some sort of Kopstootje Congress where the spoils go to the creator of the most sublime jenever-beer match. A worthy contender for that would be the Rutte Koorenwyn (from Dordrecht-based Rutte, the producer that really introduced me to the spirit) and Hamer & Sikkel Porter from Brouwerij De Molen of Bodegraven, the Netherlands. I'm glad I've procured many a bottle of jenever on my repeated trips to the Lowlands. I'm going to mad-scientist the shit out of these pairings.

Brown Cafés

I typically like to mix the new with the old when I'm visiting the Netherlands, so, for a bit of contrast with the modern craft cocktail bars, I'll almost always pop in on the traditional Dutch pubs known as brown café—so named for the tobacco stains that had accumulated on the walls over the course of many generations.

If you utter the words "brown" and "café" audibly enough for passing strangers to hear, invariably someone will volunteer, "have you been to the Dokter?"

Café De Dokter, as it's officially known, is a brown café's brown café, with an origin story that dates back to 1798. The name doesn't come from the notion that it's likely to cure what ails you—though a two-ounce pour of jenever is as good a remedy as any, as far as I'm concerned—but the fact that it was founded by a surgeon who worked at a nearby hospital. Two-and-a-quarter centuries later, the sixth generation of the founding Beems family continues to operate this local curiosity.

Measuring a mere 194 square feet (eighteen square meters for the metrically oriented), De Dokter prides itself on being "the smallest pub in Amsterdam." While I'm not 100 percent sure whether or not that's true, no one else in the city has stepped up to claim that distinction. So, let's just assume that it's true, shall we?

And, as I've noted previously, tiny bars are the best bars. They practically encourage solo sipping because it's not like they're going to be able to fit any groups in there. De Dokter might be able to squeeze in fifteen very skinny people at a time.

Another blast from the past—albeit a slightly roomier one—is De Drie Fleschjes ("The Three Bottles"), originally built back in 1650. The pub does is best to preserve the look and feel of its earliest days, with its wood floor and wall full of antique jenever bottles. It's wonderful when I'm feeling a bit peckish, thanks to the small plates of traditional snacks on offer (I'm a sucker for the little dried sausages, which pair spectacularly with the house spirits. But you can also get things like cheese and olives if you're so inclined). While there's a wide enough selection of jenevers (and a few beers for all of your koopstotje-crazy needs), as well as some lovely Dutch liqueurs (the Netherlands's other major, more widespread spirits tradition), you're going to be limited to the Lucas Bols portfolio. Bols runs the place.

Schiedam

Despite it being the most populous Dutch city and the main one that most folks outside of Europe have heard of, Amsterdam is not quite as synonymous with jenever as one might think. That distinction belongs to a much smaller—not to mention, much harder to pronounce municipality about an hour south of the capital city: Schiedam (it sounds kind of like "ski-dumb" but make the "k" in "ski" more throat-cleary). It was once the center of the jenever-making universe, home to around four hundred distilleries in its nineteenth-century heyday. In fact, the jenever coming out of the comparatively bite-sized city was once known simply as "Schiedam," much like the brandy coming out of Cognac is called cognac. It was that well-known.

Today, there are but a handful of distilleries in the city. And some of those only relatively recently rekindled the jenever flame. Gin and liqueurs tend to be their bread and butter.

Jeneverie 't Spul

But if you really want to be transported to a time when the spirit practically flowed through the streets and you couldn't spit without knocking over a glass of the stuff with your projectile saliva, then you should spend as many lazy days as possible sipping from among hundreds of varieties at 't Spul, a pub that is also a shrine to the spirit's history—especially within the context of its hometown.

I personally consider it an introvert's oasis because A) it's the very essence of "cozy," and B) there's so much to sample, learn, and quietly contemplate that you could probably leave the place with a PhD in juniper-enhanced maltwine-based spirits, and C) there's so much eye candy in the bar area that you'll be visually entertained for hours. The pub houses a grand piano emblazoned with "Steinweg," as in Heinrich Engelhard Steinweg, who emigrated from Germany to New York and became Henry Steinway. Adjacent to it sits a classic accordion. (Cabaret performances were common pre-COVID). The musical splendor continues with trumpets, French horns, trombones, a bass drum, lutes, and other vintage instruments that I couldn't quite identify.

Oh, did I mention there's also a small museum in the back room? Hundreds of bottles—some dating back at least a century and a half—assorted glassware, gadgets, trinkets, artwork, and a plethora of other artifacts and well-preserved promotional ephemera.

'T Spul owner Rob van Klaarwater was giddy when he realized that I had a passion for his local spirit (after I ordered my third glass in a succession of increasingly obscure brands), and he was more than eager to share many a story from the past four centuries of jenever history. And he couldn't wait to show me the many toys in his collection. One particularly curious item was a bottle from Bols that was on the market in the fifties, possibly into the sixties. In post-war Holland, booze companies were keen to court the American market and tried many a gimmick to lure in drinkers across the

't Spul's proud owner

pond. Bols thought a snow globe–like bottle with hourglass contours and gold flakes for "snow" gently sprinkling down upon a ballerina figuring dancing to "Blue Danube" (did I mention it's also a music box?) would do the trick.

Another item that I won't soon forget was a crankable, antique bottle washer that looked like it could double as a medieval torture device if some Renaissance Faire needed one in a pinch.

And the best part about the place is that it's but one of two jenever museums in Schiedam and it's the smallest of the two. The other is the official National Jenever Museum a few blocks away. It's a multi-floor experience that really made me feel like a kid in a candy shop who just wanted to get lost among its many delights and locked in.

It also happens to be a working distillery producing its own brand, Old Schiedam. Rutger Vismans has the best job in the world as the head distiller there, crafting several different varieties on the museum's restored late nineteenth century equipment, complete with coal-fired stills. "As they say on *MTV Cribs*, 'This is where the magic happens,'" he declares as Vismans ushers me into the old-school still-house on my private tour (the absolute best way to see any museum because of the lack of other people. No unnecessary small talk. No obligation to politely chuckle at unfunny jokes some tourist tries to make. There's also an audio tour available in four languages,

Rutger Vismans

including English, so you can really tune out the rest of the world and just immerse yourself in the spirited history. But I digress).

Since we're on the subject of magic, I really wanted to get to the bottom of what made Schiedam so special that the city's name and the spirit it produced were interchangeable.

A big part of it, Vismans tells me, is the water. Schiedam water has a high concentration of sand, which serves as a natural filter. It's not unlike the story Kentucky distillers tell about why the Bluegrass State became so famous for bourbon. It's their own limestone-rich water.

Back in the day—let's call it a century and a half ago—jenever was not only the liquor of choice in Schiedam and well beyond, but it was also a big part of the production team's compensation package. Workers were entitled to a drink every two hours—which really adds up when you consider they were working fourteen-hour shifts in those days. So, figure a two-ounce pour of the house jenever seven times a day. Ouch! And it wasn't even like they could pace themselves by gently sipping and savoring. Rutger showed me the glasses from which they would have been sipping: a conical cup atop a stem— but no base at the bottom of that stem. You couldn't even put the vessel down until everything filling it was gone. It wouldn't stand up. You'd just flip it, mouth-side down, when you were finished.

The good news: attendance records were impeccable.

"In the old days," Vismans tells me, "if you called in sick, you didn't get a drink. So, when they were a little sick, they'd still come in. Sick leave was low here."

The bad news: alcoholism. The seven-drinks-a-day was less an incentive than an enabler. It wasn't like, "Oh, if I go to work, I'll get a little treat." It was more, "When I try to stay home, I get the delirium tremens from alcohol withdrawal, which are far worse than any flu symptoms." Thankfully, no one's really drinking on the job these days. And in the off-hours, jenever fans have made moderation a big part of their lives.

I found in Rutger a kindred spirit, as he, too, enjoys some alone time between him and his glass, quietly enjoying the ritual of solo sipping.

"I sit down, relax, put my feet up, and just enjoy the drink," he says. "The first sip is top to bottom."

Wait a second, that sounds a lot like doing a shot! How is that relaxing? But that is 100 percent not what he means. It's the sensory progression of the whole ceremony. "First, take a look at the drink, then smell it, and then taste it. That's what I mean by 'top to bottom.'"

Vismans is on Team Snifter—mainly because of that second step in the top-to-bottom routine. But he admits he often pours in a little more than the serving that you'd get at a bar like Rosalia's Menagerie or 't Spul—not because he wants to get blitzed, but because he's comfortable in his easy chair and doesn't want to have to get up for a refill.

He would like to say he curls up with a good book while he's enjoying his spirit, but he admits that it's more likely he'd be watching a movie—the genre and title of which, and the specific jenever he pairs with his enjoyment of that film, depends on the mood he's in at that moment. "I have to switch it up," he says.

The same goes for his preferred kopstootje pairings. "I prefer to find a pair that suits the moment. It sounds corny, but you just have to find the right kopstootje."

The season plays a considerable role in that search.

For instance, the Bobby's brand—produced in Schiedam mere blocks from the museum at the nearly 250-year-old, continuously operating distillery Herman Jansen—sports some lemongrass and citrus character and wouldn't necessarily be the proper choice for a cozy winter night by the fire.

You're going to want to pair it with something equally refreshing and summer-friendly, like a Kölsch (if you can, get a true Kölsch produced in Cologne. If not, there are hundreds of American craft breweries that make spot-on interpretations of the style). What you're not going to want to have in the summer is a Belgian Tripel, an Imperial Stout, or something similarly chewy and boozy. Save that for those snowy evenings and match it with a jenever with a high malt content and botanicals that evoke the sort of baking spices you'd find in a Christmas fruitcake.

"A really nice thing to do," Vismans notes, "is, in the library of your own mind, try to find the beer and the jenever that you like."

And that journey is ongoing for him. The night before my museum visit, he was shocked to discover that a 0 percent ABV beer—"I was driving," he says—made a remarkable companion for the spirit he was consuming.

"The combination of flavors was spot on," he reveals. "All of the beautiful flavors came out and the acid was toned down a bit."

Part of the joy of living in modern times, during both the craft beer and craft spirits revolutions, is that there are more possible kopstootje combinations than anyone is ever likely to try in a single lifetime. "In the old days, there was just the jonge style jenever and pilsner, and people would just slam it. Not anymore."

If It's Booze Day, This Must Be Belgium

The booze world definitely needs more museums—especially when those temples of historical reflection also double as working production facilities. So, I was thrilled to learn that the Schiedam's one-two punch of the National Jenever Museum and the Borrelmuseum in the back of 't Spul are followed by a third, about three hours away in Hasselt, Belgium.

It seems that the Netherlands—fairly or unfairly—gets the most attention when it comes to jenever. I was plenty guilty for help perpetuating that myself. But it's high time that Belgium starts to get its due.

Between 2005 and 2013, I visited various parts of Belgium, each time with the same primary objective: drink as much stellar (but not Stella!) Belgian beer as possible (2nd place: eat as many frites with as large a variety of funky dipping sauces that a reasonably healthy human being can without dying). In those days I rarely associated Belgium with distilled spirits, much less jenever—which I don't think I had even heard of the first few times I landed at Brussels Airport.

Even once the spirit was prominently on my radar, my jenever-centric journeys were exclusively Holland-centric.

Fortunately, I was able to get a crash course in everything I'd been missing at Jenevermuseum Hasselt.

Like the Schiedam Museum, the Hasselt campus features a working distillery—under the supervision of head distiller Steven Reekmans—using deliberately ancient equipment. Steam power is the name of the game here, so if you're into steampunk, this could be your holy place.

In terms of overall square footage, the Hasselt site is a bit larger than its Schiedam cousin, thanks primarily to the fact that the Belgian government subsidizes it (not the case with the Netherlands institution). And I feel like Belgium owes it to Hasselt and to the spirits drinking world as penance for how unfairly the jenever industry had been treated from the nineteenth century through much of the twentieth.

As was the case in the United States at the time, the temperance lobby had grown in influence and made life hard for anyone who made their living producing or selling booze. To be fair, alcohol abuse was on the rise—or at least folks were paying more attention to it—just as it was in America. Additionally, the beer industry became an active adversary of sorts to the jenever producers, not liking to have their thunder (well, really their market share) stolen.

"The brewing industry, they were anxious about money," Jacobs reveals. "And the brewers were not as innovative, so they lobbied the government to limit jenever production." (The beer lobby there is still extremely powerful today.)

It's hard to think of Belgian brewers as lacking innovation since their traditional beer styles have been among the most revered and influential in the world, but by the turn of the twentieth century most of those styles had been pushed aside in favor of what remains the dominant category of beer in the world: pilsner. It wasn't until the mid-twentieth century that the brews we consider quintessentially Belgian started getting a meaningful revival. But that's a story for another day.

So, the nineteenth century came to a close and you don't need to tell me what happened in the second decade of the twentieth. When there's a war going on, industries like distilling tend to suffer. Trenches were dug and

much blood was spilled across the Belgian countryside. Kaiser Wilhelm II's army was eager to spill even more blood, so it confiscated most of the copper stills in Belgium to convert to materials to feed the German war machine.

Fortunately, November 11, 1918, came along and the war ended. But what didn't end was some people's insatiable desire to eliminate booze. And their wish was mostly granted, thanks to a little something known as the Vandervelde Law—a prohibition of sorts, banning high-ABV liquids (meaning spirits, of course). The law, enacted in 1919—the same year the dreaded Eighteenth Amendment was ratified in the United States, by the way—was, for all intents and purposes, Belgian Prohibition without it explicitly being prohibition. Named for Emile Vandervelde, Belgian minister of justice (and devout anti-alcohol crusader) at the time, the legislation did a number of things. It increased taxes on alcohol fourfold and effectively banned consumption of spirits in public places. And it became next to impossible for many to buy or sell it. See, if you wanted to drink jenever in the privacy of your own home, you had to buy a minimum of two liters of it at a time. "Because of the high tax, it was impossible for the common people to buy it," Jenevermuseum Hasselt director Davy Jacobs tells me at a corner table in the museum's café, which boasts the largest selection of the spirit—120 or so bottles—at any single bar in Hasselt and, quite frankly, most of Belgium.

Fortunately, there were always exceptions. Bars and cafés could apply for special dispensation to serve high-ABV drinks—a privilege that carried a significant price tag.

Enforcement was pretty hardcore in the first years following the Vandervelde Law's enactment. After it was on the books for two decades, Belgium was once again a war zone and under German occupation so it's not like the Nazis were going to let much commercial production happen anyway. But after the country was liberated and the war ended, the law softened a bit.

"[Bars] just had to buy permission and it was fine," Jacobs says. "The law just evolved."

One of the key elements that distinguished post-war Belgian jenever production from that of the Netherlands was that Belgium saw a surge in production of fruit-distillates that (confusingly) still went by the name "jenever."

"To keep their heads above water, distillers had to be creative," Jacobs explains. "Most Belgian distillers in the seventies and eighties produced fruit-based jenever. It's a phenomenon you barely see in the Netherlands."

By the late eighties and early nineties those spirits had pretty much morphed into liqueurs, neutral spirits with added fruit flavors and very low ABVs, in the 18–20 percent range. The museum café offers some of those, as it's all a part of Belgian jenever history.

At the start of the twenty-first century there weren't very many distilleries left in Belgium—Jacobs estimates that there were maybe eight to ten. Only recently, as craft distilling became an international phenomenon, did Belgium start to see some new producers pop up. The renewed interest in traditional, old-style jenever in the Netherlands spilled across the border as well.

"Nowadays, you see small, local distillers making small batches for local restaurants, local cafés," Jacobs says. "There's a focus on craftmanship."

As of 2021 there were around forty jenever producers in the country—however, Davy is quick to qualify that number by noting that only about a quarter of those produce their own maltwine. The other 75 percent purchase the distilled malt base from other makers and re-distill it or infuse it with their own botanicals.

As you'd expect, much of the enthusiasm for jenever is coming from Belgian bartenders eager to mix with the traditional regional spirit. That should pick up steam throughout the rest of the 2020s. There are few better ways to spend an afternoon—no, make that a whole goddamned day—than to stake out the corner table in the museum café and taste my way through Belgium's best. The café's open only during museum hours, 10 a.m. to 5 p.m. every day except Tuesday. If I pace myself right, I could try a new one every forty-five minutes and get through nine of those—and a good book—in a single sitting. In roughly eleven visits, I will have tasted the entire menu. I might even be able to get through the coffee-table-sized hardbound jenever history book that Jacobs and Reekmans gifted me. It's all in Flemish and it would likely take me a good couple of weeks to run every passage through my phone's Google Translate app.

Of course, there's a much easier way to immerse yourself in the spirit's centuries-old heritage. Wander around the museum, which should delight even the most scholarly of history geeks. It features the largest collection of marketing posters, some six hundred such bits of promotional artwork dating back to about 1870. Some of those included designs by arguably Belgium's most famous painter, René Magritte, who had a day job as a graphic artist before he became world-renowned.

There are also between sixty and seventy paintings from bygone eras depicting jovial bar scenes—just good folks enjoying the good life while sipping their favorite spirit. As a counterpoint, the walls also feature works of anibooze propaganda, depicting such scenes as a family torn apart by a father who drinks too much. Such images were in a similar vein to William Hogarth's famous "Gin Lane" illustration representing mid-eighteenth century London's fall into chaos and depravity thanks to the British spirit (whose roots are in the Netherlands and Belgium).

To the museum's credit, not all such works are presented mockingly. They're there as a sober (sorry, there's no other appropriate word) reminder, in the extreme, of the consequences of immoderation.

I learned more than I ever could have wanted to know about the spirit and its role throughout history—from the first applications of the juniper berry in Ancient Greece and Egypt, to jenever's earliest medicinal uses to treat upset stomachs and depression, to modern pub life. At the time I visited there was a temporary exhibition of pinball machines, highlighting the arcade games' presence in twentieth- and twenty-first-century drinking establishments. I happily raise my glass to that because pinball, after all, is a beacon for introverts in a sea of pub-based recreational activities that are designed for multiple participants.

If it all sounds like sensory overload, it can be if you don't pace yourself. Good thing there are about 120 bottled "friends" waiting for you in the café when it's time to unwind.

JENEVER CLASSIFICATIONS

There are a few things you need to know about jenever before making your selection. There are three basic styles: Jonge (young), Oude (old), and Korenwijn (grain wine). The funny thing about the Dutch spirit is it upends everything you may already know about spirits because it's pretty much the only time that "young" and "old" have nothing to do with aging. Jonge jenevers are young in the sense that the style is newer than the old/oude style. There's a higher maltwine content in oude jenever, between 15 and 50 percent. The remaining spirit is neutral.

The jonge style came into fashion in the late nineteenth/early twentieth century, as neutral spirits became more of a thing. (Think the base spirit of gin.) To be classified as jonge, the jenever's maltwine content must be below 15 percent. The vast majority of jenever volume on the market today—somewhere in the mid-to-high nineties, percentage-wise—is of the jonge variety. And much of it doesn't even come close to the 15 percent threshold. It's not uncommon to find something whose maltwine concentration is under 2 percent. That's changing slowly as the younger generations discover jenever and Dutch craft distilleries get in touch with their heritage and produce more oudes.

As for Korenwijn—the non-neutral malt content is much higher, usually between 51 and 70 percent. It's not technically a jenever because it doesn't have to contain any juniper whatsoever.

There's also a niche, unofficial classification of Moutwijn ("maltwine") jenevers, which can contain up to 100 percent maltwine—similar to the way the spirits were way, way back.

Jenever-based Cocktails

Philip Duff, the man behind Old Duff Jenever, offered up a few of his faves. This first one, created at The Connaught Bar in London by mixologist Ago Perrone and his team, is quite a journey, combining so many disparate ingredients that somehow work exceedingly well together.

GATE NO. 1

Serves: 1

²/₃ ounce Old Duff Jenever

²/₃ ounce London dry gin

1 teaspoon peated Islay single malt Scotch whisky (Laphroaig and
   its ilk)

3 teaspoons sweat vermouth

²/₃ ounce pinot noir

²/₃ ounce port

2 teaspoons milk jam*

1 ounce strawberry-basil kombucha

Ice (enough to fill the mixing glass)

Chocolate gate (for garnish)

Stir all ingredients together in a mixing glass and garnish with a
chocolate gate.

---

*   You probably don't have milk jam just laying around your house, so here's a
relatively simple recipe for that: Bring 1¼ cups sugar, 1 quart milk, ½ vanilla bean
(halved lengthwise and scraped), and 1 teaspoon baking soda to a boil in a saucepan
over medium to high heat. Stir constantly to dissolve the sugar (similar to the way
you would when making simple syrup). Reduce heat to low and let simmer for about
2 hours until you get a thick, spreadable consistency. Make sure you scrape the sides
and bottom of the pan every 15 minutes or so. When finished, pour through a fine
strainer to remove any remaining sediment, then let cool. You won't need too much
for this drink, so you'll have plenty left over to spread on toast or spoon over ice
cream. You won't regret it!

THE KINGSMAN

Serves: 1

Narthan McCarley-O'Neill of The NoMad Hotel in New York developed this one using a 100 percent maltwine spirit, so you're going to get a sense of the Dutch distillate in all its grainy glory.

1 ounce Old Duff Jenever 100 percent maltwine

½ ounce rye whiskey

½ ounce Oloroso sherry

¼ ounce blanc Agricole rhum

1 barspoon banana liqueur

Ice (enough to fill the shaker)

1 oversized ice cube (for the glass)

½ ounce brown-butter fat-washed falernum*

In a cocktail shaker, stir all ingredients, then strain into a rocks glass over a single oversized ice cube.

---

* For the brown-butter fat-washed falernum, toast 3½ ounces unsalted butter in a pan until it's light brown. Stir with a full 750-ml bottle of falernum. Bottle mixture in plastic, seal, and place in a freezer for 24 hours. Strain the liquid through a fine mesh filter.

FANCY KEY

Serves: 1

Here's another one out of New York, this time from Ali Martin from The Up & Up. Very spirit-forward.

¾ ounce fuscia Old Duff Jenever

1 ounce cachaça

½ ounce Braulio amaro

¼ ounce funky pot-still Jamaican rum (such as Smith & Cross or The Funk)

1 ounce coconut mix*

Ice (enough to fill the shaker)

Crushed ice (for the glass)

2 spritzes absinthe, 1 mint spring, and grated chocolate (for garnish)

© Matt Piacentini

In a cocktail shaker, shake all ingredients hard and strain into a brandy snifter full of crushed ice. Add more crushed ice to make a dome and insert straw. Garnish with absinthe, mint, and grated chocolate.

_____

* For the coconut mix, combine two parts Coco Lopez coconut cream with one part coconut milk.

TOP GUN
VOLLEYBALL SCENE

Serves: 1

Ali Martin has one more for us. The name is pretty self-explanatory. This one could get a little complicated, especially since it requires an iSi whipped-cream canister.

2 ounces fuchsia Old Duff Jenever*

1 ounce citric acid**

1 ounce simple syrup

1 ounce chilled fizzy water

3 ounces saison-style beer

1 dash rose water

1 dash salt solution

16 drops Bittermens Celery Shrub

Stir all ingredients together. Bottle, seal, and chill in the fridge. Drink straight or over ice.

---

*   For the fuchsia Old Duff Jenever, place 2 cups Old Duff 40 percent ABV Jenever, 1 ounce black currant tea, 2½ ounces grapefruit peel, 12 ounces watermelon, and 1²/₃ ounce lime peel in an iSi whipped-cream canister, seal, and "charge" with nitrous oxide. Leave for ten minutes, swirl, then gently release the gas. Strain the liquid through a fine mesh filter.

**   For the citric acid solution, stir 1½ ounces citric acid into 30 ounces water until fully dissolved.

MOONLESS SKY

Serves: 1

Credit for this entry goes to Arlene Wong of The Pontiac in Hong Kong, China. It's definitely a lot simpler than the others, with fewer esoteric ingredients to chase. And it's quite the pick-me-up.

½ ounce Old Duff Jenever

1½ ounces coffee liqueur

½ ounce blanco/blanc vermouth

1 barspoon rich simple syrup (2 parts sugar to 1 part water)

Ice (enough to fill the shaker)

Coffee beans (for garnish)

In a cocktail shaker, shake the ingredients hard and strain into a chilled cocktail coupe. Garnish with coffee beans.

The next few recipes are from Tess Posthumus, owner of Flying Dutchmen Cocktails and Dutch Courage in Amsterdam. This is the former venue's house drink, hence its name.

© Ming Chao

FLYING DUTCHMEN COCKTAIL

Serves: 1

This is the first drink I had when I visited its namesake bar. Here's what Posthumus had to say about her creation: "This cocktail is a real crowd pleaser. All ingredients represent our bar and Dutch (drinking) history. For example, the basis is our traditional jenever and the orange cocktail bitters give a nod to the Dutch royal family and the traditional drink for 'royal celebrations,' orange bitter liqueur. The orange flower water hints at our famous export product: flowers. Speculaas is a spice mix that originates from the ancient spice routes and the addition of gum arabic (gum arabica) is a traditional way of making syrup from the bartending world, which provides a wonderfully coating mouthfeel."

1½ ounces Bols Barrel Aged
    Genever
1 ounce lemon juice
15 milliliters speculaas-gum
    syrup*
2 dashes orange bitters

1 dash orange flower water
Ice cubes (enough to fill the
    shaker)
Orange twist and edible
    flower (for garnish)

Add all ingredients to a cocktail shaker. Shake hard and strain into a prechilled coupe glass. Garnish with an orange twist and edible flower.

---

*   For the speculaas-gum syrup, mix ¼ ounces gum arabica with 200 grams sugar. Dissolve gum-sugar into 350 milliliters water over heat. Don't let it come to a boil. Strain and set aside. Then, toast ⅓ ounce cloves, 1 teaspoon nutmeg, 1 teaspoon white pepper, 1 teaspoon green cardamom, and 1 teaspoon peeled and chopped ginger in a large pan. Add in 150 milliliters water and 350 grams sugar and mix until sugar is dissolved. Don't let it come to a boil. Add this spiced syrup mix to your gum syrup mix. Heat again and add 450 more grams sugar. Let it dissolve and cool back to room temperature. Fine-strain and store in a clean glass bottle for up to 3 months in the fridge.

KESBEKE MARTINI

Serves: 1

Posthumus puts an innovative twist on this often taken-for-granted classic.

40 ml jenever (preferably young-style)

40 ml dry vermouth

5 ml pickle brine infused with clove and star anise

Cornichon (for garnish)

Combine and stir all ingredients. Strain into a coupe glass and garnish with a cornichon.

© Ming Chao

© Ming Chao

ZILT

Serves: 1

This Dutch spirit gets a slight Spanish accent in Posthumus's next creation.

- 2 ounces jenever (preferably old-style)
- 1 teaspoon PX sherry
- ½ teaspoon salted muscovado syrup (2 parts muscovado to 1 part water with a pinch of salt)
- 1 dash Fee Brothers Black Walnut bitters
- Cubed ice (to fill the glass)
- Orange twist and salted and caramelized walnut (for garnish)

Combine all ingredients in a mixing glass. Stir and strain into a rocks glass over cubed ice. Garnish with an orange twist and a salted and caramelized walnut.

DUTCH COUPE

Serves: 1

Posthumus concocted this one in honor of Dutch Queen Beatrix abdicating the throne back in 2013. She voluntarily resigned and passed the crown to her son, now King Willem Alexander. "As the drink also comes in a coupe glass, I thought the name 'Dutch Coupe' would fit perfectly," Posthumus explains. "It's a slightly bitter drink with orange notes and jenever based—jenever as it's the spirit of the Netherlands. Try to use an aged old jenever or corenwyn-style jenever, as the drink needs the malty backbone to support the other ingredients. I've included orange because our royal family is called 'van Oranje', the House of Orange. Back in the day the Dutch would drink oranjebitter at royal celebrations, which is a bitter orange liqueur. So, this celebration cocktail needed to have some bitter notes as well. Inspired by Ada Coleman's Hanky Panky, another great woman in history, I think this drink is fit for a queen. The only thing missing was Queen Beatrix's feathery hat, a signature of hers. So, try to replicate this by garnishing the Dutch Coupe with a pretty 'feathery' orange zest."

2 ounces Bols Barrel Aged Genever

½ ounce Carpano Antica Formula

⅓ ounce Cynar

1 dash orange bitters

1 dash orange flower water

Orange twist (for garnish)

Combine all ingredients and stir. Strain into a coupe glass and garnish with a pretty orange twist, fit for a Queen.

ORIGINAL MARTINEZ

Serves: 1

The Martinez is a nineteenth-century cocktail that's said to be the precursor to the martini. Many believe that jenever, not gin, was the original base ingredient.

2 ounces Smeets Whisky Cask Jenever or any oude (old-style)
    jenever with a high maltwine content

1 ounce sweet vermouth

1 teaspoon Maraschino syrup

1 teaspoon dry Curaçao (Pierre Ferrand, for example)

1 dash bitters

Ice (enough to fill the mixing glass or shaker)

Orange twist (for garnish)

Chill a coupe or tulip glass. Combine all ingredients in a mixing glass or shaker and stir for about twelve to fifteen seconds. Remove the ice and strain into the glass. Garnish with an orange twist.

Since Hasselt is the historical center of Belgian jenever culture, I consulted with a local bartender there to get some recipes. Rob Biesman from the city's Koks & Tales had these next few recipes to offer up.

© Jon-Pierre Pijls

BEAUTY AND THE BEAST

Serves: 1

Ice (enough to fill the glass)

1 ounce Smeets Extra Jenever

$^2/_3$ ounce Smeets Berry Jenever

$^2/_3$ ounce lime juice

1 dash orange bitters

2 ounces Fentiman's Lemonade (to top off)

1 whole fresh crimson rose (for garnish)

Fill a highball glass with ice. Pour jenevers, lime juice, and bitters over the ice, then top off with lemonade and give a brief stir. Garnish with a crimson rose. Present the drink on a wooden coaster under a globe or dome if possible for dramatic effect.

BEER 'N' OIL

Serves: 1

Ice cubes (enough to fill the glass)

2 ounces barrel-aged jenever such as De Moor Founders Reserve
   12 years

1 ounce Big Daddy's Falernum

2 teaspoons lime juice

2 dashes Angostura bitters

1 dash soy sauce

Lime wedge (for garnish)

Fill up a rocks or Old Fashioned glass with ice cubes. Pour in all the liquids. Stir for 10 seconds, add more ice if necessary, and garnish with a lime wedge.

CLAM MARTINI

Serves: 1

This one's a bit more complicated, but well worth it, especially if you're into shellfish.

Crushed ice (enough to fill the mixing glass or shaker)

2 teaspoons dry vermouth

2 ounces young Jenever ('t Stookkot, Smeets, De Moor, Ketel One)

2 teaspoons pickled clam or mussel brine*

1 dash Boker's Bitters

Ice cubes (enough to fill the mixing glass or shaker)

Lemon twist

Pickled clam or mussel on a toothpick (for garnish)

Chill a martini glass. In a mixing glass or shaker, pour in crushed ice and dry vermouth and stir for about 15 seconds. Discard everything in the glass/shaker (you just want to give it a rinse with the vermouth). Now, add the other liquids and lots of ice cubes to your mixing glass and stir for another 15 seconds. Strain into your chilled glass, squeeze in a lemon twist, and garnish with a pickled clam or mussel on a toothpick.

---

* For the brine, heat a pan with a tiny bit of olive oil and add chopped onions and celery and a handful of clams or mussels and season to your liking. Cook for two minutes, add 3–4 ounces white wine, 2 ounces white wine vinegar, a bay leaf, some cloves, and juniper berries. Then, strain the mussels or clams from the liquid, remove the shells, and let both of them cool down. Once cooled, put the deshelled fish back together with the liquid in a jar and keep refrigerated. It will keep for a week.

EMERALD ISOLATION

(ALONE IN IRELAND)

Anyone involved with booze in the United States knows that we love to romanticize the illicit past of some of America's distilling traditions. In the modern legal industry, moonshine has become a successful category unto itself, harnessing the outlaw legacy of generations gone by. (At the end of the day, though, it's really just unaged whiskey or other spirit that hasn't spent any time in a wooden barrel. Yay, marketing!)

I can only imagine that the ghosts of long-dead Irish distillers are watching over some of their twenty-first-century US-based counterparts and saying, "Heh. You're adorable."

That's because you can't really talk about moonshine without mentioning "poitin," a spirit whose production in rural parts of Ireland, many believe, dates back as far as fifteen hundred years—not entirely likely, but never let the facts get in the way of a good story—and has spent most of the past four hundred of those being illegal. In the mid-sixteenth century, Parliament decided it wanted to start requiring a license to produce the stuff and about one hundred years later, in 1661, the Brits banned it completely. It wasn't about protecting the people and reigning in the scourge of liquor production. It was about money.

You see, it was easier to collect taxes on distilling activities in urban centers like Dublin, Cork, Belfast ,and Derry than it was out in the farm lands—where most of poitin-making was happening. Britannia was always at war with someone—most often the French—and those conflicts weren't going to pay for themselves!

This ruling certainly didn't stop the country dwellers from making the stuff. It drove such activities deeper underground. In fact, much of what the farmers were producing was often superior to the output from the big-city distilleries—primarily because the former didn't have to cut corners on quality to afford to pay the still tax and remain profitable (because they were hiding their stills and ducking the tax!).

The name poitin derives from pota, which means "little pot," as in pot still—distinct from the large stills that the urban mass producers were using. It's as simple as that. The legal, big-city stuff became what we now know as whiskey. Poitin makers applied the derogatory nickname "Parliament whiskey" to the stuff coming out of places like Dublin, just to underline how beholden the "legitimate" distillers were to the British powers-that-be. Like whiskey, poitin's traditional base ingredient has been barley—though crops like potatoes and sugar beets had been used as fermentation substrates from time to time. Poitin had also been known to be a considerably higher proof than whiskey. You could call it Irish moonshine, as many do, but that would be doing it a disservice since its existence predates, by at least several hundred years, the first known use of the term describing illicit alcohol in the United States.

Flash forward to 1997 and poitin production becomes legal for the first time in 336 years. And like its formerly forbidden American counterpart it is, for all intents and purposes, an unaged whiskey (except it's more likely to be made from barley—both malted and raw—than it is from the preferred, but by no means exclusive, stateside ingredient, corn).

While many examples of modern, legal poitin retain the ultra-proof tradition of their ancestors, a growing number have dialed it back a bit, putting it more in line with the 80ish proof common among whiskeys.

The desire to taste some twenty-first-century poitin varieties fueled my solo trip across both the Republic of Ireland and Northern Ireland, hiding from society much like seventeenth-, eighteenth-, nineteenth-, and twentieth-century producers hid their stills from the government.

To get a taste of a representative cross section of poitin from producers across Ireland, I knew I had to pop in on Bar 1661 in Dublin, named for the year poitin was made illegal. The owner, Dave Mulligan, is one of his country's greatest ambassadors for the spirit (I first met him presenting a session on poitin at the San Antonio Cocktail Conference). Bar 1661 offers the

widest selection of poitin in one place, with around forty different bottles at any given time. As I stared at the menu, I felt like Ralphie when he was waiting in line to meet Santa in *A Christmas Story*. "Leave me alone, I'm-a, I'm thinking."

I started with some Mad March Hare, a brand that has the widest availability (still extremely limited) outside of Ireland. I noticed the somewhat sweet aroma right away and when I sipped, I got elements of nuts and, strangely enough, some vanilla. Usually, a barrel would impart the vanilla notes, but this is completely unaged and never spent a minute in wood.

Next up was Ban Poitin (pronounced "bawn"), a brand launched by Mulligan himself, along with cocreator and fellow poitin evangelist, Cara Humphreys. Ban was noticeably more complex. A great deal of peppery spice asserts itself, along with some very distinct, bakery-evocative nut-like graininess. It's like dipping a crusty bread into black pepper–infused olive oil. It's got a fairly innovative composition as well. Instead of just a barley base, its mash bill combines that grain with potato and molasses.

I also had the opportunity to try a peated version of Ban, which would please any fan of an Islay whisky. Mulligan finishes the spirit in Laphroaig casks, so you know you're going to be in for a treat. That's not to say it's a smoke bomb. Quite the contrary, the peat smoke is surprisingly subtle, mostly expressing itself on the back end. Up front, I got a lot of a Grape Nuts-esque cereal character. Mulligan is doing the Lord's work!

My flight continued with Northern Ireland's Killowen, which has a delicate combination of malted barley, oats, and wheat in its mash bill. The wheat softens the intensity of the barley a bit and the oats give the poitín a subtle creaminess. It's certainly one I wanted to take my time with because it was incredibly nuanced, thanks to the interplay of the disparate cereals.

My final selection is the one that inspired me to travel clear across Ireland—granted, it's only a two-and-a-half-hour train ride from the East to the West Coast—to Galway to see where the stuff is made and spend time in a bite-sized distillery when no one else was there. The spirit in question is Micil (pronounced "Mick-ill"), from the distillery of the same name. More on that in a moment.

I wasn't quite ready to leave Bar 1661—not before I had the pub's signature boilermaker. Honestly, I can't remember an instance when I was more transported by a simple beer-and-shot combo. It was Ban poitín and the most stunningly poured pint of Guinness I've ever seen in my life. The poitín just makes the roasted notes of the Guinness build and build until they completely engulf you. It was nothing short of sublime and this grain-a-palooza made me a true believer.

If you're looking for as authentic a poitín experience as you can get, you can't do too much better than the Micil Distillery in Galway, on the western coast of the country. Pádraic Ó Griallais opened the distillery in 2016, but he's drawn upon six generations of family distilling tradition in the Connemara region of the country, beginning with his direct ancestor and distillery namesake Micil Mac Chearra, who commenced his spirits-making career in 1848. And that spirit, of course, was poitín. Pádraic exudes not only familial pride, but an intense regional affection as well, distinguishing the Connemara spirits-making heritage from that of the rest of the country. And he's one of the best historians on local distilling history—both illicit and aboveboard.

Pádraic Ó Griallais

He'll be the first to tell you that, historically, the west side of the country was where most of the poitín-making activity was concentrated. Parliament whiskey was more the norm in the south and east—even though now, Mulligan's predominantly poitín-focused bar is in the eastern capital city.

The poitín maker's instinct to hide from the world is alive and well at Micil, mainly because the distillery is extremely difficult to find. It's tucked away in the back of a venue called Oslo Bar in the Salthill section of Galway, barely half a block from the ocean. The bar is vast, spanning two large rooms, and you have to walk through both of them before you reach Micil. That was enough to make me fall in love with the place.

The tasting room is a shrine to the history of the family's and the region's poitín-making past, with an ancient, wooden still in the middle of the floor (the actual operating stills are in the actual stillhouse in the next room). Ó Griallais poured me samples of the range, including the flagship poitín I'd sampled at Bar 1661 the night before, as well as the special, peaty Heritage Edition and Micil Gin (it pays the bills).

The Heritage Edition starts spicy and fruity before the peat kicks in on the nose. It reminded me of barbecue rub, with a chipotle or paprika-like accent. I mentioned that the peated Ban would appeal to Islay Scotch whiskey drinkers. I'd bet that the Micil Heritage Edition would be quite attractive to mezcal aficionados.

A component that sets Micil apart from its peers is the infusion of bogbean, a local botanical that brings bona fide terroir to the recipe.

I wish I could've set up a cot and moved into the Micil Distillery. It's just the sort of secluded bunker or panic room, within the madness of a popular hot spot, that I'd love to call home. And I've got bottles and bottles and barrels and barrels of poitín to keep me warm.

Seriously, though, what I really wanted to do was experience poitín out in the wild and I encountered a few opportunities to do just that.

Before I caught my train back to Dublin, I dropped in on King's Head pub. Its generic name was enough to make me want to walk on by, but, thankfully I didn't. It was the perfect midday escape. It was quiet, the music was at about a "two" or "three" on my scale (Lorde's "Royals" was about as energetic as it got), the walls were stone and cellar-like, the requisite antique stove was right next to me, and tea lights encased in lanterns illuminated the place. It had an expansive whiskey list, but I wanted my last taste of Galway to be poitín. And King's Head more than delivered with both of Micil's signature poitíns. I had the classic, non-peated one on the rocks as I toasted farewell to the west.

When I got back to Dublin, I found myself caught in the tractor beam of a speakeasy. Yes, I know I've had some unflattering words about other venues within that genre, but Dublin's the Blind Pig gets a pass—which, I admit, is odd because I've always found speakeasies in countries that didn't deal with Prohibition to be a bit ridiculous.

Blind Pig definitely amps up the mystery—you don't know the address until you book a reservation (with a ten-euro deposit, which is applied to your order). Unfortunately, Google maps spoils the fun. Just type in "Blind Pig" and you'll find out exactly where it is. But you still won't get in because you don't have a reservation. So, play along, okay?

The bar's in the basement of an Italian restaurant (and serves some food items off of the restaurant's menu). A fake wall hides the drinking establishment and to enter you have to press a bronze pig's head. But that's where the kitschy speak-easiness of it ends.

I've always bemoaned the "fake Irish pubs" in the US and, I guess, Ireland has every right to fight back with their own versions of American bar traditions. But the Blind Pig doesn't want to replicate the hackneyed trappings of a stateside speakeasy. No, the bar truly makes the concept its own. It's inside an old underground stone arch, which evokes more medieval dungeon than 1920s jazz club. The city has the benefit of some gorgeous, authentic architecture and I'm glad the Blind Pig is able to take advantage of that. The only feature that was decidedly American was the fact that the speakers had blues emanating from them (at a delightful "two").

Candlelight sustains the mood and kept my corner table dark enough for me to melt into the shadows. It was there that I deliberately nursed one of the most radically iconoclastic cocktails I'd ever had. It was called a carrot and stick and included turmeric-infused Ban poitín, Crème de Banana, cardamom, carrot juice, orange soda, and sour orange juice. As weird as that may sound, it gets even weirder when I tell you I paired it with some meatballs. The whole experience was unforgettably delicious. The servers were beyond helpful and friendly. I was the only solo drinker in there and they bent over backwards to make me feel welcome, comfortable, and not like I was doing anything out of the ordinary. The place is obviously a stellar first-date venue, but tonight, and throughout this journey, I was on a date with myself.

And I thoroughly enjoyed the company.

Poitín-Soaked Potions
Mad March Hare is among the modern, completely legal poitín brands that are building a presence not just in Ireland, but in the United States as well. The producers were generous enough to share a few of their favorite cocktails that showcase this enigmatic spirit.

THE CHICKEN, THE EGG, AND THE HARE

Serves: 1

The egg white brings a nice frothiness to this floral-sweet-sour symphony.

1⅓ ounce Mad March Hare poitín (or similar brand)
⅔ ounce Elderflower Liqueur (St-Germain, for instance)
⅔ ounce lemon juice
⅓ ounce egg white
⅙ ounce simple syrup
Ice (enough to fill the shaker and the glass)
Lemon wedge (for garnish)

In a cocktail shaker, shake all ingredients and fine-strain over ice in a rocks-style glass. Garnish with a lemon wedge.

THE WILD FRIAR

Serves: 1

This one's a nice balance of bitter, sweet, and sour, with a greenish hue, thanks to the Chartreuse.

$5/6$ ounce Mad March Hare poitín (or similar brand)

$5/6$ ounce Lime juice

$5/6$ ounce Chartreuse

$5/6$ ounce Maraschino syrup

Ice (enough to fill the shaker)

Lime peel (for garnish)

In a cocktail shaker, shake all ingredients and fine-strain into a prechilled martini-style glass. Garnish with a lime peel.

BLOODY MOONEY

Serves: 1

I'll use any excuse to get to include an offbeat riff on a Bloody Mary.

$1^2/_3$ ounces Mad March Hare poitin (or similar brand)

5 ounces tomato juice (as always, I'm partial to juicing a can of San Marzano tomatoes)

2 dashes Worcestershire sauce

1 dash Tabasco Sauce (or other hot sauce)

$^1/_2$ ounce celery liqueur (try Apologue Celery Root Liqueur for something intriguingly complex)

Ice (enough to fill the glass)

Celery stick, lemon or lime wedge, and 1 pinch freshly ground pepper (for garnish)

In a cocktail shaker, shake all ingredients and pour into an ice-filled glass (a pint glass works fine). Garnish with a celery stick, lemon or lime wedge, and top with a pinch of pepper.

MAD DOWN SOUTH

Serves: 1

Here's a reimagined mint julep with an Irish accent.

1²/₃ ounces Mad March Hare poitin (or similar brand)

1 spoonful mint jelly

¹/₃ ounce maple syrup

⁵/₆ ounce lemon juice

Crushed ice (enough to fill the glass)

Add poitin, mint jelly, maple syrup, and lemon juice to a julep cup half-filled with crushed ice. Churn and top off with more crushed ice.

MIDNIGHT MADNESS

Serves: 1

Espresso martinis are all the rage. But trust me, this is much better.

1⅓ ounces Mad March Hare poitín (or similar brand)
⅓ ounce Kahlua
⅓ ounce Frangelico
1 ounce espresso
Ice (enough to fill the shaker)

In a cocktail shaker, shake all ingredients and fine-strain into a prechilled martini-style glass.

MICIL MULE

Serves: 1

Ice (enough to fill the glass)
1½ ounces Micil Poitin
4 ounces ginger beer
Lime wedge (for a "good squirt" of lime juice)

Fill a glass with ice. Pour in the poitin and top off with the ginger beer. Squeeze in the lime wedge.

EPILOGUE

PANDEMIC HANGOVER

We've spent the majority of this book exploring the best sorts of places to drink alone—or with the smallest group of people that is humanly possible (which usually means alone, but okay, you can bring a close friend)—but I haven't focused much on the venues to avoid like the plague. And speaking of plagues, I kind of had this epiphany at a time when the world was fully reopening as more than half of the US population had received their COVID jabs. New York and New Jersey were among the last American holdouts to lift all restrictions, so it was kind of a big deal to be drinking indoors, once again, in Jersey City—my former home on the western bank of the Hudson River, right across from Manhattan. I first moved there in 1999 and by the time I finally left in early 2015, its bar scene had started to rival that of Williamsburg and Bushwick, Brooklyn.

I'm not going to name the particular cocktail-centric establishment at the heart of this forthcoming anecdote because it's generally a good place—just not for me—and quite popular. I'd only been there a couple of times previously, as it opened a year or so after I moved away, but I usually enjoyed myself. It was probably due to the fact that it has an extensive spirits list, well beyond the usual suspects.

However, on this most recent visit I didn't even get to *see* said list, on account of the fact that the bar was still employing the scan-the-QR-code-and-see-our-menu-on-your-smartphone technique of performative safety protocols. Sure, it's always great to err on the side of caution and eliminate as many touch points as possible in the name of sanitation, even though, by that point (summer 2021), it was pretty common knowledge that COVID wasn't really transmitted via surfaces. (That's not to say I'm not fastidious about sanitizing surfaces. Even pre-pandemic, I was wiping down my tray table, seatbelt, seat, and the back of the seat in front of me every time I got on a plane. I'm more concerned about catching colds!)

Listen, I've got no beef with virtual menus, especially the ones that let you order and pay right from your seat without having to deal with another human being (save for the runner). Even the ones that don't offer that option are perfectly fine with me—under one condition: the bar has to have Wi-Fi.

I'm no diva. Ninety percent of the time I'm on the 5G network, happy to burn through my monthly data allotment because it's pretty substantial and I rarely go over. However, when I can't get a signal in certain locations—which is common in restaurants and bars located in basements or those in brick city buildings that are sandwiched between other brick city buildings, especially in the seats farthest from the street.

And that's exactly the problem with the bar in question. I went at opening time, 5 p.m., on a Monday because I knew there'd be the fewest people to deal with then. And I was right. For the first forty-five minutes or so, it was just me and the bartender, who, for about twenty of those forty-five minutes kept asking me what I'd like to order. I wasn't being indecisive, I was trying to get the fucking menu to load because I was down to less than one bar on my phone.

"Do you have Wi-Fi?" I asked. "No, sorry," replied the barkeep. "Well then it's going to be a few more minutes before I decide what I want because there's no signal in here." He shrugged and walked away.

Eventually I gave up and went with my usual go-to, the Old Fashioned. I know, I know, you're going to say, "But you said early in the book that the Old Fashioned is the only cocktail that needs to exist." And you would be correct. But at this particular juncture, I wanted a neat pour of whiskey or brandy—preferably one I hadn't tried before—and it was too dark to see what bottles were behind the bar (also, I'm tremendously near-sighted and had put off an appointment to get my eyeglass prescription updated; my last pair stopped working for me around 2016 and I haven't worn them since).

As someone who's always encouraging people to get out of their comfort zones—especially when drinks are concerned—I was crestfallen, having been forced to retreat into mine. That's not always a bad thing. Sometimes when we're in new, unfamiliar surroundings, comfort booze can serve as our True North when we've been knocked off balance. It's a good first sip.

Unfortunately, I had to remain in that zone for my second order as well because the signal situation had not improved. But since I was determined to have a neat pour of bourbon—on what just happened to be National Bourbon Day—I was squinting to see if there were any familiar bottles seven feet in front of me. Luckily, I recognized that most iconic of bottle shapes, the rhombicuboctahedron (I had to look that up), that is the glass container housing what is, in my opinion, the bourbon lover's sipping bourbon: Blanton's.

Speaking of that tragically overused word, "iconic," I'm going to help further beat it into the ground by applying it to the vessel in which my Blanton's pour was delivered: the contoured Glencairn glass. (I challenge you to find a better glass for nosing and tasting whiskey!)

By then, someone else had come into the bar, sat two stools down from me, ordered a cocktail, and clinked glasses with me when she received it. It dawned on me then that I was being a bit of an asshole complaining (to myself, of course. I would never unload on a server because their boss is too shortsighted to make a passworded Wi-Fi network available to guests). The "cheers" was a moment few have been able to enjoy for nearly a year and a half. I was drinking one of my all-time favorite whiskeys, in my all-time favorite drinking vessel for such spirits, *inside* a bar, toasting the stranger nearest me.

I was able to forget my gripe for a couple of minutes.

That doesn't mean I'm going to let this go!

There's this smug attitude pervading certain corners of the hospitality world where it's frowned upon to be looking at your phone. Many establishments often go so far as posting signs on the wall that read something to the effect of: "No, we do not have Wi-Fi. Stay in the moment. Pretend it's 1995."

I get it. I'm all about the whole "be here now" philosophy (or at least I'd like to be. My anxiety usually forbids it). But that's all well and good if you're hanging out with one or more other people. You've already got your conversation partner. When you're alone and you need to tell a friend something or ask a question, your only recourse is to text them.

There doesn't even need to be a social aspect to that screen time. All QR menus aside, the phone provides a very necessary service for many of us—and I'm not talking about ordering your Uber ride home. For me, it's frequently an educational drinking companion. When I encounter a new brand or cocktail, I want to learn as much about its style and backstory as possible. Unless the bar has a full-time sommelier that can be talking to twenty

guests at the same time—spoiler alert: it doesn't and it never will—I have no other option than to dive down a series of Internet rabbit holes and satisfy my boozy curiosity. And those portals lead to others and, before I know it, I've learned the entire history of Romanian distilled beverages and the bar is about ready to close. For an introvert, that's a stellar night out. We're not out to get hammered, we actually want to learn things about what we're drinking. And, in the process, we're going to learn about drinks we didn't even know we wanted and we're probably going to order that next. If you're a bar, that means more money in your pocket. So please, for the love of God, don't give us the stink-eye when we're looking at our phones (unless it looks like we're on a date and ignoring our companion. Then you can throw us the hell out).

You never know. We might be in the middle of posting a review about how great your bar is and would you really want to stop us from doing that? Or we could be texting a half-dozen friends, inviting them to join us, and therefore, potentially putting more money in your pockets.

In any event, anything short of us coming into your establishment, fileting a rainbow trout we just caught, eviscerating a wild boar we just shot, or generally harassing the staff or other guests should not be your concern, as long as we keep paying for our drinks and behave in a respectful manner. Introverts like to make our own fun and as long as you keep letting us, we'll keep supporting your business and encouraging others to do the same.

So, when you see us sitting alone, scrolling through our phones, staring into a book, or simply staring into space, contemplating the world, feel free to raise a glass in our general direction.

Just don't try to make small talk.

ACKNOWLEDGMENTS

I never know where to begin these things and I know I'm probably going to accidentally leave someone out, so I apologize in advance! Just know that it really does take a village to put something like this together.

I want to give a hearty shoutout to my agent, Max Sinsheimer, who convinced me that, of all the insane ideas I pitched as my sixth book, *Imbibing for Introverts* was the one to do. I especially thank him for dealing with all of my whining. And extra special thanks to my editor Leah Zarra, for believing in this project and being incredibly patient. And I extend that thanks to everyone at Skyhorse.

And to Elena Makansi, for the gorgeous illustrations that really brought this project to life.

To my wife, Craige Moore, for your patience, love, and understanding, even when I wasn't clearly communicating on which continent I might be at a given moment.

To Mike, Sue, and Dave Mansbridge, for guiding me through the real England and for the best ploughman's lunch I've ever had. You all went above and beyond, and I am eternally grateful.

To Rachel Bonnewell, Pepijn van Beusekom, Wouter Bosch, and everyone at Rosalia's Menagerie, past and present, for always making me feel at home and for expanding my Dutch drinking education.

To Tess Posthumus for the jenever cocktail contributions, for creating Dutch Courage and the Flying Dutchmen, for the conversation, and for generally geeking out over jenever with me.

To Davy Jacobs and Steven Reekmans at the Jenever Museum in Hasselt for making me fall in love with the beverages of Belgium all over again.

To Rutger Vismans at Jenever Museum Schiedam, for showing me around and giving me the "kid in a candy shop" experience.

To Chris Franjola for putting some can't-miss Los Angeles dive bars on my radar.

To the mixtresses, Sonia Worcel and Catherine O'Brien, for so many generous and innovative cocktail concoctions that truly enhanced this book.

To Philip Duff, for pointing me in the right direction throughout Holland, setting up so many meetings, and giving me a treasure trove of recipes.

To Amber Gallaty for doing the same for Ireland, for really helping to immerse me into the poitin world, kind of like the way I accidentally immersed myself in Annapolis Harbor when I was borrowing your stand-up paddle board.

And speaking of poitin, to Dave Mulligan, for devoting a whole bar to the stuff and for guiding me through the Irish spirit.

To Markus Suttle, for hosting me for the happiest of happy hours at said bar.

To all the human beings I could tolerate enough to have drinks with: Christine Deussen, Lew Bryson, Stephen Lyman, Christopher Pellegrini, Beth Gerbe (who, I hope, loves Katana Kitten as much as I do), John Holl, Jon Page, Joe Orlando, Clare and Adam Sivits, Sarah and Giancarlo Annese, Karen Auerbach, Roland Ottewell, and to the "Supper Club": Schuyler, Farshad, Gilman, Francis (and, of course, Craige).

Like I said, I'm probably pissing many people off by not mentioning them, but I'll buy you a drink, I promise!

CONVERSIONS

(These conversions are rounded for convenience)

Ingredient	Cups/ Tablespoons/ Teaspoons	Ounces	Grams/ Milliliters
Fruit, dried	1 cup	4 ounces	120 grams
Fruits or veggies, chopped	1 cup	5 to 7 ounces	145 to 200 grams
Fruits or veggies, puréed	1 cup	8.5 ounces	245 grams
Honey, maple syrup, or corn syrup	1 tablespoon	0.75 ounce	20 grams
Liquids: cream, milk, water, or juice	1 cup	8 fluid ounces	240 milliliters
Salt	1 teaspoon	0.2 ounce	6 grams
Spices: cinnamon, cloves, ginger, or nutmeg (ground)	1 teaspoon	0.2 ounce	5 milliliters
Sugar, brown, firmly packed	1 cup	7 ounces	200 grams
Sugar, white	1 cup/ 1 tablespoon	7 ounces/ 0.5 ounce	200 grams/12.5 grams
Vanilla extract	1 teaspoon	0.2 ounce	4 grams

INDEX

Note: Bold entries indicate photos.